Peter Ackroyd was born in London in 1949. He is a graduate of Cambridge University and was a Mellon Fellow at Yale. He has been literary editor and managing editor of the *Spectator*, for which magazine he is also film critic. He also reviews television in *The Times* and books in the *Sunday Times*, and broadcasts and writes frequently elsewhere.

Peter Ackroyd has previously published two volumes of poetry, three critical studies and, most recently, his first novel, *The Great Fire of London*, which is also available in Abacus.

'. . . a compulsively readable faction.' *The Bookseller*

Peter Ackroyd

THE LAST TESTAMENT OF OSCAR WILDE

An Abacus Book

First published in Great Britain by Hamish Hamilton Ltd 1983
Published in Abacus by Sphere Books Ltd 1984
1st reprint 1984
2nd reprint 1985
3rd reprint 1987
4th reprint 1988
5th reprint 1989
6th reprint 1990

Printed and bound in Great Britain by
BPCC Hazell Books
Aylesbury, Bucks, England
Member of BPCC Ltd.

ISBN 0 349 10059 4

Sphere Books Ltd
A Division of
Macdonald & Co (Publishers) Ltd
Orbit House
1 New Fetter Lane
London EC4A 1AR
A member of Maxwell Macmillan Pergamon Publishing Corporation

For Audrey Quinn

9 August 1900

Hôtel d'Alsace, Paris

This morning I visited once again the little church of St Julien-le-Pauvre. The curé there is a charming man who believes me to labour under a great sorrow; once, he approached me on silent feet and whispered as I knelt before the altar, 'Your prayers may be answered by God's grace, monsieur.' I told him – I could not whisper – that my prayers have always been answered: that is why I come to his church each day in mourning. After that, he left me in peace.

It is not generally known that St Julien tired of his mission somewhat early in life. He healed the maimed and the sick, but they reviled him because they could no longer beg; when he cast out devils, they simply entered the bodies of those who watched the miracle; when he prophesied, he was accused of spreading disillusion among the rich. So many times was he turned away from the gates of great cities, so often did he ask for a sign from God which God would not send, that he gave up his ministry in despair. 'I have been a healer and a prophet,' he said. 'Now I will be a beggar.' But a strange thing occurred: those who had scorned his miracles then worshipped his poverty. They pitied him and, in their pity, they made him a saint. His miracles have been forgotten absolutely. This is the saint for me.

As I left the little church this morning, three young Englishmen passed me. I have grown accustomed to such encounters, and adopted my usual posture. I walk very slowly and take care not to look in their direction: since I am for them the painted image of sin, I always allow them the luxury of protracted observation. When they had retreated to a safe distance, one of them turned around and called back at me, 'Look! There goes Mrs Wilde! Isn't she swell?' I walked on with flaming cheeks and, as soon as they had turned the corner of the rue Danton, I hastened back to m

1

room here, my nerves quite ruined. I still tremble as I write this. I am like Cassander of the pantomime, who receives blows from the harlequin's wand and kicks from the clown.

During the terrible days of my trials, a letter was delivered to me: it contained only an illustration of some prehistoric beast. That was how the English thought of me. Well, they tried to tame the monster. They locked it up. I am surprised that, on my release, the London County Council did not hire me, to be fired from a cannon or perform acrobatic tricks at the Tivoli. The monstrous is terrible – Velasquez knew this when he painted his dwarves – but ugliness and wretchedness are trivial merely.

The simplest lessons are those which we are taught last. Like Semele who longed to see God and was wrapped in fire which consumed her, so I longed for fame and was destroyed by it. I thought, in my days of purple and of gold, that I could reveal myself to the world and instead the world has revealed itself to me. But although my persecutors have tormented me, and sent me into the wilderness like a pariah dog, they have not broken my spirit – they could not do that. Since I was driven in a closed cab from the gates of Reading prison, I have been freed in ways that I could not then have understood. I have no past. My former triumphs are of no importance. My work has been quite forgotten: there is no point in instructing Romeike's on my behalf, for there will be no cuttings. Like the enchanter who lay helpless at the feet of Vivien, I am 'lost to life and use, and name and fame'. It fills me with a strange joy. And if, as my friends say, I am Hindoo-like in my passivity it is only because I have discovered the wonderful impersonality of life. I am an 'effect' merely: the meaning of my life exists in the minds of others and no longer in my own.

So it is that the English treat me as a criminal, while my friends continue to regard me as martyr. I do not mind: in that combination I have become the perfect representative of the artist. I have all the proper references. I am Solomon and Job, both the most fortunate and the least fortunate of men. I have known the emptiness of pleasure and the reality of sorrow. I have come to the complete life – brilliant success and horrible failure, and I have attained the liberty of those who have ceased to develop. I look like Mrs Warren but without, alas, the profession.

I have in the past been called worse things: imprecations have been taken from the pit of Malebolge and hurled at me. It no longer matters what name I carry – Sebastian Melmoth and C.3.3.

have been convenient for dramatic purposes, and both of them seem quite appropriate when my own is a dead thing. When I was a boy I took enormous delight in writing it down – Oscar Fingal O'Flahertie Wills Wilde. The whole of Irish legend lies in that name, and it seemed to bestow power and reality upon me. It was the first proof I ever received of the persuasive powers of literature. But I am tired of it now and, sometimes, I recoil from it in horror.

I picked up the *Mercure* the other day, and it was there in the middle of a paragraph of unbearable French. I put down the newspaper as though it were in flame. I could not look at it. It was as if in that name, Oscar Wilde, there was a void in which I might fall and lose myself. A madman sometimes stands on the corner of the rue Jacob – opposite the café where I sit. He cries out at the cabs as they pass by and spatter him with mud. No one could know so well as I the agony and bitterness that force him to speak in bewildered words. But I have learned the simple lesson: I am one of the damned who make no noise.

The whole course of my former life was a kind of madness also, I see that now. I tried to turn my life into a work of art. It was as if I had constructed a basilica upon a martyr's tomb – but, unfortunately, there were to be no miracles. I did not realise that then, for the secret of my success was that I believed absolutely in my own pre-eminence. When I gilded each day with precious words and perfumed the hours with wine, the past and future seemed to be of no account. I must connect them with simple words: I owe that to myself. Now that I have seen my life turn completely in its fiery circle, I must look upon my past with different eyes. I have played so many parts. I have lied to so many people – but I have committed the unforgivable sin, I have lied to myself. Now I must try to break the habit of a lifetime.

When Maurice arrives with today's news of the boulevards, I shall inform him of my new resolution. I shall have to impart the news to him gently; if the dear boy comes in to find me at my desk, he will die of shock. I have allowed him to believe that my only interests are the ones which he shares. If he discovers that I have begun a journal, he will write at once to Robbie Ross accusing me of seriousness and other unnatural vices. Of course he does not understand literature. He asked me once who 'Mr Wells' might be. I told him he was a laboratory assistant, and he went away much relieved.

Maurice is a wonderful friend. I met him by absurd chance. I happened to be in the bookshop behind the opera-house when I saw him scrutinising the shelf devoted to modern English literature. I knew from long experience that a volume of my *Intentions* lay there, and I waited impatiently to see if he would take it down. Alas, he opened something of an explicit nature by George Moore.

I could restrain myself no longer, and I approached him. 'Why,' I asked, 'are you interested in that particular author?'

Maurice was quite unabashed. 'I live by the café where he says he learned French, the Nouvelle Athénes.'

'Well, it is a disgrace that such a place is allowed to remain open. I shall speak to the authorities about it tomorrow.'

He laughed and I knew at once that we were going to be great friends. He told me that his mother was French and his father English, but that his father was dead. It is true, I said, that English people tend to die with unerring regularity. He was astonished by my candour. Of course he did not know who I was: his father had not mentioned my name to him, not even on his death-bed. But I can forgive anything of those who laugh, and I decided to educate Maurice myself. I introduced him to my friends and, occasionally, I allow him to buy me dinner.

On these summer afternoons we lie on my narrow bed and smoke cigarettes. He has heard from the wind and the flowers that I was once a great writer, an artist of international reputation, but I do not think he believes them. Sometimes in an unguarded moment I will describe a fiery-coloured scene from *Salomé* or repeat a more than usually apposite epigram. Then he gives a curious side-long glance as if I were speaking of someone whom he does not know.

'Why do you not write now?' he asks me.

'I have nothing whatever to say, Maurice, and in any event I have said it.'

In the spring More Adey was with us. He had brought over a volume of my poems to present to me. It had only just survived the sea-crossing. I really did not want it, and I raised my hands in horror.

'But, Oscar, some of these are quite remarkable poems.' More always talks like a solicitor – except when he is soliciting.

'Yes, More, but what do they mean? What do they mean?' He looked at me, and could not think of an answer.

4

I can of course begin this apologia with some confidence. De Quincey has done it, Newman has done it – some people say that even St Augustine has done it. Bernard Shaw does it continually, I believe – it is his only real contact with the drama. But I must discover a new form. I do not want to write in the style of Verlaine's confessions – his genius was to leave out anything that might be of the slightest possible interest. But then he was an innocent – in the proper sense of that word, he could do no harm. He was a simple man forced to lead a complicated life. I am a complicated man enmired in the simplicity of a dull one. There are some artists who ask questions, and others who provide answers. I will give the answer and, in the next world, wait impatiently for the question to be asked. Who was Oscar Wilde? All I need now is the overture to *Tannhaüser*. Here comes Maurice: the heavy tread suggests important news.

10 August 1900

Gide once told me that he kept a journal: what little there is in it must, I imagine, be of a sensational nature. I will attempt something in a more educational vein: I have already designed the frontispiece.

THE MODERN WOMAN'S GUIDE
TO OSCAR WILDE

A Romance

'I owe everything to it.' Mr Bernard Shaw

'I always consult this book when I travel.' Mrs Patrick Campbell

Only one copy will be printed, on Japanese vellum, and exhibited in the Natural History Museum.

11 August 1900

What captivity has been to the Jews, exile has been to the Irish. For us, the romance of our native land begins only after we have left home; it is really only with other people that we become Irishmen. I once said to William Yeats that we were a nation of brilliant failures: but I have since discovered that in failure there is a great strength to be earned. The Irish nation has sought its bread in sorrow; like Christ it knows how weary the way has been and, like Dante, how salt the bread when it has been found – and yet out of these sufferings has sprung a race of incomparable poets and talkers.

Of course exile, for me, has been a life-long romance. If I did not always bear the mark of the leper on my brow, as I do now, I have never ceased to carry the mark of Cain in my heart. And yet it is one thing to feel distinctive and so to walk apart, quite another to know that one is alone. When I climb the dark staircase of my hotel, I recall with the poet how steep are the stairs in houses of exile. Once the world watched me in amazement; now it has let me go, and does not care which direction I take in my wanderings. Goethe said of Winckelmann, that great scholar who abandoned the sombre house of his native culture for the free light of Hellenism, that 'the image in which one leaves the world is that in which one moves among the shadows'. Well, then, I shall be a perpetual *boulevardier* watching the angels – I presume there will be angels – hurrying by.

I would go mad if I sat in this room for too long, among the relics of my former life. Regret and remorse rise up in front of me and the sight is intolerable: I flee from the hotel like a guilty thing and enter the streets. I walk joyfully through them only because I do not know where I am going – although sometimes, I believe, my companions do. It is remarkable how interesting life becomes when one has ceased to be a part of it. In the old days, when my personality was the golden chain which bound me to the earth, the world seemed unreal, a painted scene against which I stood in relief like a satyr upon an Attic vase. Now it seems to me to be perpetually bright, renewed daily, quite meaningless in its expense of daily activity but wonderful nonetheless – as long as one does not care to pierce its mystery. And yet even this tires me: I can do nothing for very long. As a dramatist I looked upon other people as sources of amusement or pleasure; now they crowd around, and jostle me. It is as if their own personalities invade me and leave me exhausted: I know that it is only in the company of others that one becomes truly oneself, but now I am positively Whitmanesque. I contain multitudes. Although I possess the wonder of Miranda, I have also the faintness of Prospero who foreswears his art as soon as life has quite matched his expectations.

I believe that poverty is responsible for my remarkable gift of passive contemplation. I used to think that the only way to waste money was to save it; I did not know that, when one no longer has green pieces of paper in one's pocket, one has nothing. Only the other day I was forced to borrow a few francs from Maurice – he had news only of Dreyfus, so I refused him lunch – simply in order to leave my room. I ask for money because I deserve it and yet friends insist that they have none to give me, that I must learn to work again. Poverty teaches many bitter lessons, but the hardest is that revealed in other men's hearts. I still recall a terrible scene with Bosie, last month, outside the Café de la Paix.

'Alfred,' I said in a perfectly friendly manner, 'I need your help.'

'When you call me Alfred, I know you want money.'

'Alfred, Bosie dear, I am about to be thrown out of my hotel.'

'Why? Did the boy make too much noise, or did you?'

'That is unworthy of you. You know how I hate to discuss matters of finance –'

'Only when they concern yourself, Oscar.'

'Please, Bosie, do not violate our friendship with words of scorn.'

'Our friendship, as you call it, was violet from the beginning.'

I had quite forgotten that he aspired to being a poet.

'Quite frankly, Bosie, I need the money. I need it desperately. I have left my clothes at the Hôtel Marsollier and the proprietor threatens to sell them if I do not pay what is owing to him.'

'Oscar, you used that excuse last month.'

'Oh, did I? I had forgotten, I am so sorry. It shows the utter collapse of my imagination under the influence of penury. Nevertheless my situation never changes, Bosie, I am depending on your good will.'

He took out from his pocket some franc notes, threw them upon the ground, and left the café, shouting as he did so, 'You know, Oscar, you have the manners of a prostitute.'

I picked the notes up at once, and ordered another drink. Do you find this dishonourable? Well, then, you see to what a pass I have come. When you can no longer change the world, the world changes you. The poorer I become, the more terrible Paris seems. I shall have to hide in one small corner of it soon, I see that now, or else it will overwhelm me. When Bellerophon was thrown from Pegasus by Zeus, who envied his transports, he was suddenly forced to contemplate the details of a thorn bush: I may have to become reconciled to my wallpaper.

But, if poverty leads to contemplation, contemplation guides one towards sloth. Idleness is the supreme condition of the artist, but idleness must walk with joy. When idleness exists merely, apart from joy, then, in Bunyan's charming phrase, one is 'the robin with the spider in his mouth'. Only the memory of my art lingers, like shades around my head. I may wander among the living but, since Apollo killed me, my soul has already travelled down to the Asphodel Fields. The beautiful Roman word *umbratilis* is perhaps closest to my condition, but I do not think the Romans would apply it to me. At most I might play a role in one of Plautus's more horrifying comedies. I might be the old lecher, his face painted and his hair dyed, who is an object of ridicule to the audience whenever he appears – although the audience does not know that it is laughing at itself. The world always laughs at its own tragedies: it is the only way it has been able to endure them. Now I am going for a walk.

I decided to take the omnibus instead: I have an especial affection for the ill-starred 13 which travels between the Place Clichy and the Palais-Royal. I sit on the top of it and look out – a modern city should always be seen from the air; sometimes I even listen to what is being said. The French have tried to turn conversation into an art, but their language lacks the darker shades which bring speech to life. English, for example, is

9

remarkable for the number of colour words with which it can express gloom – they are quite unknown in French. Baudelaire was responsible for adding despair to the French tongue, but he succeeded only in being euphonious.

But I digress into matters which no longer concern me. Now, like a Cook's traveller, I am forced to see the world. I sit in cafés for hours at a time and watch people whom, before, I would not even have considered momentarily. Every small gesture interests me, and from the face or manner of each person I invent an entire history. For the first time I have noticed the lost and the lonely – how, with their curious apologetic gait, they move through the world like strangers. And I weep. I admit it: I weep.

There is a passage in one of Balzac's novels where he describes the poet as one 'who seems to be doing nothing but nevertheless reigns over Humanity once he has learned to depict it'. Indeed it is possible that a new form of drama might be created out of the ordinary talk and gestures of the people – and, when I sit in a café and watch them pass, I imagine a miracle through which all of their sounds and movements could be turned into a strange, multi-coloured art. But I do not think it is my role to create the drama or literature of a new age: I can manage Lamentations, but not Revelations.

I have called myself idle but, really, I am not a prey to idleness but rather to stupefaction. Only Edgar Poe has properly understood the lethargy of the will, the curare that annihilates the nervous elements of thought and motion. Will was always an important element in my success: like Lucien de Rubempré in that terrible moment of self-knowledge, when he realised that the heart and the passions of the heart had nothing whatever to do with his genius, I, too, sacrificed everything to the fame I saw approaching me. Of course one is always given what one needs, not what one wants – that was my great miscalculation. Or perhaps life has been finally revealed as Poe himself knew it to be, although I took care not to know it myself – we do not understand what we really want, and so we proceed by indirection or by chance to the goal which is already hidden within us.

That would be the most terrible irony of all – that my success and my fame were but small staging posts on my grand journey to infamy and, finally, to oblivion. I am neither in Heaven nor in Hell. I am, as Dante said, *sospeto*. I explore my position with some interest.

13 August 1900

I woke this morning, just before dawn, and the pain in my head was so intense that it seemed to me then that it might be my last morning on earth. At first I felt afraid, but then I was filled with a strange joy. What wonderful things I might say! But, when I made the slow descent into my personality, it was as if I had been struck dumb. I could hear the sound of the vegetable carts driving over the cobbles on their way to Les Halles, and the sound was as deadly to me as the executioner's cart which Villon heard in the dungeon of Meury. But pain has not provoked in me the fiery life which Villon found. I have nothing to say: if this were indeed my last morning, I could declare only that I heard the vegetable carts of Paris arriving at such-and-such an hour. That is all. It is scarcely enough to appear in volume form.

All powers of imagination have deserted me now. When I wrote in my glorious days, it was joy which led me forward and joy which revealed the world to me; even in prison, joy returned when I wrote my long letter to Bosie. Now it has gone – in that terrible phrase, 'the waters have flowed over my head' – and I don't care to struggle in order to regain it. When I left prison, I wrote my Ballad to demonstrate to the world that my suffering had served only to improve me as an artist. I planned then, after the Ballad, to return to the Bible and find there the great dramatic themes which contemporary Europe has quite forgotten: I wished to turn the history of Jezebel and Jehu into a work of art as suggestive as my *Salomé*. But my plans decayed as soon as they were conceived. My will faltered, and was gone. I shall not accomplish the work I want to do, and I never will. And how useless regret is – my life cannot be patched up, that is all. At least I have the consolation that I shall not appear in Mr Walter Scott's 'Great Writers' series.

Yet the death of an artist such as I am is a fearful thing. Death itself holds no terror for those who have known and understood life, but to lose one's powers as an artist – that is the unendurable punishment. On me has been visited the doom of the Phrygian Tantalos, to see the fruit and be unable to taste it, to have wonderful visions and then be forced continually to forsake them.

Of course my friends do not realise this: they believe that literature resembles an unfinished letter, which can be taken up at any point. Robbie Ross writes to me as if he were Miss Marbury, the American 'agent', and sometimes I suspect that he is. He orders me to begin a new play but I have explained to him that I cannot do proper work outside England. Now I write only for the more advanced schoolboys; they send me their photographs, and ask advice about the production of my plays. I reply in scarlet form. I am a Silenus to whose feet the cherubs come. Perhaps I might begin a new career touring the schools of England and lecturing the young on the influence of architecture upon manners – prison taught me a great deal on that particular subject. I would create more sensation in the classrooms than Matthew Arnold. He was impossible. I am rather better, I am merely improbable. The boys understand that, and no doubt it is right that they should be interested in my work – I have always been interested in them. But the relationship has altered somewhat: they are now my peers. Society passed sentence on the artist; the coming generation will pass its own sentence on the society which did so. In them my work may live.

As it is, the modern world has no use for me. When I walk into places of public entertainment where English tourists gather, I am often asked to leave and, when in hot confusion I retreat, the curious crane their heads to look at me. If I wish to enter a restaurant, I am careful that I go only to one where the patron knows me and I eat – at table d'hôte prices – at a separate, alien table somewhere near the kitchen. Then one knows what it is to be alone. The English have always objected to my presence but now, in crowds, they have the cowardice visibly to show it. If I go to the theatre, even among the French, I am forced to sit in the cheapest seats. I go to fashionable places only when accompanied by rich friends – the English will always bow to wealth.

I am used to such behaviour from them now. Shaw has given the best definition of an Englishman. It occurs in one of his plays – I forget which, but I remember that we travelled to the suburbs in order to see it, just a few friends gathered together. 'The Englishman,' he said, 'will do anything whatever in the name of principle.' It is a perfect remark, and Shaw forgot only to add that the name of that principle is self-interest.

Once, when I was in the Café L'Egyptien, smoking what I believed foolishly to be an Egyptian cigarette, an Englishman spat at me. It was as if I had been shot. I started back, and lost all powers of speech and thought – but not, alas, of feeling. When one is the object of general obloquy, the constant fear is not when such attacks might occur, but how they will manifest themselves. I used to think that self-consciousness was a wonderful thing: I raised a philosophy upon it which turned the world into a multi-coloured cloak which the true individual places around his shoulders. But the cloak became a net as fatal as that which Clytemnestra held out in front of her. Half the power of my thought came from my vanity – when the vanity goes, to be noticed or marked out is to become lesser rather than greater.

And so now customarily I dine alone, or with those gamins who are entirely the creation of Victor Hugo. Their company entrances me because they see the world as it really is: as a result they understand me perfectly. I think that, to them, I have told my most perfect stories; since most of them can neither read nor write, I become positively Homeric. They bay for stories of love, and then they weep for me; they ask for stories of wealth and palaces, and I weep for them. We have a most satisfactory relationship. There is one café where I sit with the public executioner. Of course he does not know who I am – executioners are never interested in police records – but we play cards together. My most poetic moments come when he exclaims, 'Je coupe!'

But if it still offends me that I am snubbed by members of the English public, what is harder to endure is the sensation of being cut by other artists. I was sitting outside the Grand Café some weeks ago, when William Rothenstein passed my table – he stays in Paris when London grows tired of him. He saw me, but he looked through me: it was absurd of him, a young man, to snub the poet who created him, who showed him how to attain the personality of an artist where before there had only been certain raw – very raw – materials. But I once said that the art of life was the art of defiance: I took off my hat to him, and wished him good morning. There must have been serpents beneath that hat, since Rothenstein turned to stone.

There have been others, also. I came face to face with Whistler as he was leaving Poussin's one evening, and he ignored me. He

13

looked old and tired, exactly like one of Cranach's Virgins. Even Beardsley avoided me in Dieppe. I am told that he blames me for the entire collapse of his career. It is unworthy of him: an artist always suffers in one way or another, and it is absurd of him to heap his own pain upon my shoulders.

I understand the English, however – they are an open secret – and it pains me more when I think of my French friends who have abandoned me in their own city. Pierre Louys, Marcel Schwob, Mallarmé – none of them cares to visit me now. Even Gide crosses the street when he sees me approaching. He sent me a letter, just after I had returned to Paris from my wanderings in Dieppe, saying that he had decided to burn the pages of his journal for that one fiery-coloured month we spent together, some eight or nine years ago. I repaid the compliment by burning his letter. I believe Gide tells all his acquaintances that I was, in those triumphant years, positively Satanic – well, if I was, I found in him a willing disciple. Poor Gide, he has the face of a seducer and the manner of a virgin perpetually being defiled.

Of course I can accept the verdict of my equals such as Whistler; I have followed a life which is unworthy of an artist, and those who love the things of art and the imagination can never forgive me for what I have done. But to be cut by those like Gide who, artistically, are beneath me – well, there is no parallel in history.

Yet to be turned on by those who knew me teaches a bitter lesson in understanding. To a large extent, I realise now, my power – and the power of my personality – depended upon my position in society. As soon as that position was taken away, my personality counted for nothing whatever. In similar fashion, I once saw reality from a great height since it was from the pinnacle of my individualism; now I have fallen so low that reality rises above me, and I see its shadows and its secret crevices. The fact that I discovered within myself the strength to continue my life, that I have raised myself from humiliation in order to face the world, is a standing reproach to the modern age.

And so now my presence makes people uneasy: I am Lazarus come from the dead to mock those who buried me. Yet in my darkest hours it seems to me proper that I should be shunned, like an unclean thing. More wrote recently to tell me that Arthur, my manservant, had killed himself. Against him, too, the world turned – he was too close to me, and he suffered for it. For the curse I carry within me is greater than any which my century has conferred upon me. I have destroyed every life that I have touched – my wife, Constance, lies dead in a small grave near Genoa beneath a stone which bears no trace of my name; the lives of my two sons have been blasted, my name taken from them also. And my mother – I killed her as surely as if I had stabbed a knife in her back. I killed her and, like Orestes, I have been pursued by the Fates. I carry a strange doom with me everywhere: those whom I have touched have borne the scars of that touch, those whom I kissed have been scalded. Even Bosie, who in his poetry might have touched the heavens, has been worn to a disastrous shadow: I see nothing ahead of him but pain and weariness. And, if anyone were foolish enough to write my biography, then the fatefulness of my life would touch him, also. There will, in any event, be no royalties.

It is no comfort to me that the man who sought to encompass my ruin has himself been destroyed – Queensberry died earlier this year, and I am told that on his deathbed he spat at his own son and then called out my name in his final agony. I truly live in the tears and pain of others. And yet I shall not kill myself. Although the second Mrs Tanqueray has made suicide respectable, I shall not follow her example. I shrink from pain; and to die at my own hand is a homage to my enemies which I shall never make.

I am what I am: there is nothing more to be said. I believe there is a line to this effect in *Dorian Gray*. That odd little story was meant to be taken quite literally: it is about the corruptibility of art, not the corruptibility of the artist. It was a stroke of genius to place the canvas in the schoolroom; that is where all our troubles start.

14 August 1900

Agnes, the daughter of M. Dupoirier, the proprietor, awoke me this morning by banging on the door and shouting 'M. Melmoth! M. Melmoth!' It was a telegram merely, but Agnes has a great respect for modern communication. I had expected something Greek and simple from Bosie, but it was an ugly message from Frank Harris. KYRLE BELLEW CLAIMS PLAY – PLEASE EXPLAIN. Frank continually accuses me of selling my scenario of *Mr and Mrs Daventry* to others. He is rehearsing his own adaptation of it now and seems to be in some confusion of mind: art, and the ideas of art, are the property of no one, unless it be Calliope. If people pay me for weaving them my fantasies, I am hardly the one to prevent them. In my poverty, I have been forced to sell the imagination which was once my birth-right. Now Frank claims it as his own. I shall send a telegram back: I AM SICK AND IN PAIN. EXPLANATIONS WOULD KILL ME.

I shall sign it 'Sebastian Melmoth' – I am known in the hotel by that title simply to prevent consternation among post office messengers. When I left prison I knew that Oscar Wilde was a name which would be, in Villon's phrase, 'du charbon ou du pierre noir'. I thought of other possibilities – but Innocent XI and Oedipus were somewhat too dramatic. And so I chose the name of Melmoth the Wanderer, damned, a thing of evil. It is strange how it inspires more confidence in tradespeople than my own.

Although now I laugh at the book which carries that name, once it terrified me. My mother was the niece of Maturin, the Irishman who composed that fantasy: his bust dominated the hall of our house in Merrion Square. When I was a small child, I always averted my face from it: it seemed an accursed thing, for the marble visage had no eyes, only the lidless sockets of those whose sight has turned inwards, and been blasted by what it saw.

16

Sometimes, in the evening, my mother would read to us from that book. She sat in a low chair, and my brother, Willie, and I would lie on the floor beside her; the faint, musty smell of the carpet and the whisper of the gas when it had been turned low acted on me as a narcotic. I quite remember the horror I felt when she declaimed, in that voice which was peculiarly like my own, those passages which haunt me still: 'Where he treads, the earth is parched! Where he breathes, the air is fire!' Then she would clutch the long, velvet curtains behind her and pull them across her face. Willie would laugh – he never suffered from any excess of imagination – but I would creep towards my mother's legs, seeking comfort yet afraid to touch her when she was so transformed. Willie would beg her then to read the conclusion, and she would tell us how Melmoth the Wanderer returns, 'an object of terror and wonder to the world'. I think now that I took a curious pleasure in being frightened, and I believe my mother enjoyed frightening me. And so, naturally, I have taken the name.

I realise now, of course, that Melmoth was an outcast not because he had committed purple, unforgivable sins but because, in the weary infinity of his wanderings, he looked from a great distance at the customs and ceremonies of the world. He saw them rise and fall, and he saw them change utterly. He understood the makeshift, painted pageant of the world – and it was because of that knowledge that the world could never forgive him or let him rest. It is a mistake to demonstrate to others that their ideals are illusion, their understanding all vanity. For then they will crush you.

It is maintained by Helvétius that the infant of genius is quite the same as any other child. I do not believe so: from the earliest time I felt myself set apart. I was unworldly, more given to contemplation than to action. As a boy I was fitful and discontented, full of misery and unexplainable high spirits. My mother used to tell me, in later years, that I laughed often in my sleep – 'The Boy Who Laughed In His Sleep' would be a perfect subject for Millais – but I remember nothing of that. I can recall only those sad, grey-coloured days when I would lie on my bed and weep.

Those moods have vanished with silent feet. I have always loved children, and I believe that it is my own forgotten childhood that guides me towards them – as if I might recover in their faces and their voices the innocence which I cannot now recall. There are some writers who, with every appearance of sincerity,

17

remember with great clarity their early years: perhaps it was the only period when they showed any signs of imagination. But I am not one of these: only certain scenes and images, like the muddy vistas of Impressionist painting, now return to me.

I had few friends, and I do not believe that my family encouraged me to make any. I was one of those children who are fascinated by their own solitude – I found in it an echo of the solitude from which I knew I had come. And so I would wander, finding patterns in the cobbles beneath my feet, speaking out loud the strange phrases which would occur to me. Dublin was in the Fifties and Sixties already a decaying city; like an old prostitute, it had long ago lost its virtue and was in danger of losing its income. But I would walk through its streets quite unaware of the poverty and wretchedness around me, yet deeply moved by my own melancholy state.

The object of my solitary quest was always St Patrick's Cathedral; it was a source of wonder to me that this blackened, monstrous thing rose up among the smoking rookeries which surrounded it and that, once within its massive doors, the shrieks and the calls from the Liberties were drowned in its silence. It was my first intimation of the terrible consolations of the religious life. I would stand in front of Dean Swift's memorial, with its wonderful words, and dream that one day they might crown my life also.

Since I was so young, I walked unmolested through the narrow streets of destitution: precisely because I did not fear them, they could do me no harm. Only once was the charm of ignorance broken for me. I was walking back to Merrion Square. I had just reached the Castle when a young girl ran out of a dark court which I had just passed, and snatched the grey cap from my head. I called after her, and I was immediately surrounded by a group of urchins who jeered at me. Such scenes have become familiar to me now, and I experience still the cold moment of horror which afflicted me then. I did not know what to do: I was seized with fear and wept as they tossed the cap from hand to hand. In order that they should not see my tears I ran and, as I ran, a leg came out and tripped me. I lay upon the muddy ground, not daring to rise.

And then I felt a hand upon my shoulder, and a boy of my own age helped me to my feet. I can recall his face even now: he was one of those rare spirits in whom the fund of human kindness had not been exhausted by the misery in which he was compelled to live. He told me not to mind the boys, if they acted naughty. And he sat and talked with me, on the rough doorstep of a squalid dwelling. He knew our house and, often, he told me, he would walk in the 'gentle quarter' and peer in through the windows. He asked me how much the house cost a week – one shilling, two shillings? I said that I did not know but that it was more, much more, than that.

He fell silent, and I felt ashamed. He picked up my cap from the muddy street, handed it to me, and solemnly wished me good morning. I do not know if he was awed by my family's wealth, or whether he considered me a liar, but he went on his way, that quiet and gentle boy, through the terrible rookeries of Dublin. He walked away slowly. I wished to run after him, but some feeling of shame prevented me. I have been searching for that boy all my life.

If my mother had known of my expeditions into the Liberties, she would have forbidden them. Her nationalist sympathies extended, I believe, only as far as Grafton Street. And I would not have disobeyed her: she was the dominant note in my life. At dinner, she would allow me to sit under the table beside her as she talked to her guests. I recall still the warmth and comfort of her scented dress as I placed it against my cheek, and it is mixed in my memory with the rise and fall of her conversation. One evening she leant down to whisper to me, 'Your father has been made a knight.' When I remained stubbornly silent, she hauled me out from beneath the table, to the amusement of Sir William Wilde and the others round the table. I would not look at them. I would not even look at Sir William.

When I close my eyes, I always see my mother in the same position. I see her peering into the mirror which hung in the hall, adjusting her cloak on which Celtic images had been embroidered, wrinkling her nose as if in contempt at herself. She was a large woman who always seemed aware of her stature. She would, in the evenings, sometimes wear a purple brocaded gown, with a yellow lace fichu crossed on her breast and fastened with a gold brooch. I was fascinated by her jewellery: she had large bracelets of silver and ivory, and wore rings on every finger. Sometimes she would take my head in her hands, and I could feel the hard metal upon my cheek.

She was often in the highest spirits, and would dress me in her hats and earrings, laughing all the while, but sometimes she was wrapped in so pensive a mood that she neither saw nor heard me. I would gaze up at her as she continued her slow walk from room to room – sometimes calling out 'Mama!' – but she simply passed me by. She had certain catchphrases which would escape from her in sighs at the most improbable moments. 'Waste! What a waste it all is,' she would exclaim for no apparent reason, and then she would hum a fierce tune to herself.

On many occasions, she would come into my small bedroom and recite to me from her own work. She read to me passages from her translation of *Sidonia the Sorceress*, or from her ballads, and the music of patriotism thrilled me. 'Young Irishmen,' she would say and put her face so close to mine. 'And isn't that what you are?' Sometimes I could smell the sweet alcohol upon her breath – since that time, it has always seemed to me to be the natural companion of poetry.

In the days of my innocence all literature affected me. There have been no more pleasurable sensations in my life than those of my youth when all afternoon I would lie in bed, with a sheet over my head, reading a book which I had discovered in Sir William's library. There was always the musty, slightly sour, smell of the crinkled pages and the strange detritus which would float from their binding onto my wrist; but, principally, it is the softness and the secrecy of those silent hours which I have ever since associated with literature.

For it was at that age that I discovered poetry and in that discovery found myself. There was one book that changed me utterly. I had picked up by chance a volume of Tennyson; I was reading it in bed in that quiet hour when I should have been asleep, the lamp turned so low that the page was in shadow only. My eyes raced across the page, hungry for the immortal food which alone could satisfy it, when I came across one phrase – 'And the wind took the reed tops as it went'. I do not understand why it affected me in so extraordinary a manner: it was as if I had been aroused from some long sleep. I spoke the line aloud and got up from my bed. I stood in my room, wide-eyed. For, if I had woken from sleep, it was only to enter a longer dream.

I went downstairs to the room in which my mother was sitting. I must have looked aghast because she got up and walked towards me. I think she must have asked me what had happened, but I could not have replied. It was as if, in that wonderful phrase, someone had wiped my lips of speech – just as the milk that was wiped from Hermes' lips was scattered into the heavens and became a constellation. For I knew that I wanted to be a poet, and it was then that my destiny was cast among the stars.

From that time longings were aroused in me which I could not satisfy. I felt a certain restless dissatisfaction with all whom I met. I felt, even then, that I had that within me which would make me greater than they – and amongst the writers and artists of Dublin who visited my mother I felt a boyish, instinctive rebellion.

To my mother I turned for comfort. On many evenings she would come to my bed and lie beside me, and then I felt a strange joy which, even now, disturbs me. Sometimes she would fall asleep, and I would move closer to her and put my arms around her. I would feel her breathing, and match the rhythm of my breath to her own until I, too, slept. In the morning, always, she was gone and we resumed then the cheerful intimacy of our companionship. We were accomplices in a life which to both of us became a game. Together we would walk round Merrion Square, in stately procession, and my mother would whisper scandalous comments about those whom we passed and greeted. 'Wicked,' she would say of some inoffensive old woman, 'perfectly wicked.' 'Look at that hat he is wearing, Oscar,' pointing to a man on the other side of the street. 'It looks like a concertina. I will go and ask him to play it.'

My brother, Willie, sensed the bond between my mother and myself and, it seems to me now, disliked us both for it. Generally he ignored me, but he was older and stronger than I and in moods of anger he would kick and goad me into tears. In our early years he thought himself my superior and so became patronising; but, when I experienced my first success, his lofty manner turned to envy and sometimes bitterness. It was quite natural that when he came to London he should have become a journalist. And here is a secret: I have always suspected that he harboured the same Greek inclinations as myself but that he was too weak to yield to them. That is why he revelled in my tragedy.

It was he who five years ago turned away visitors from the door of my mother's house in London, where I sought refuge between my trials: I believe he thought they would comfort me. When my mother had retired to her room he would drink in his usual, primitive fashion, and ask the most revolting questions about my private conduct: really, it resembled a scene from Ibsen. But he is dead now – if he is not preserved in spirit, he may at least still be preserved by it.

21

Willie disliked me also because of my love for our younger sister, Isola. She died when I was twelve. Often we would play together. I would pretend to her that I was our mother: I would crane my neck and roll my eyes. I would tell her stories, the sole charm of which lay for me in the fact that she believed them entirely. When she died, I suffered from a grief so intense that it surprised even me. She was the only member of my family for whom love was not a cause of shame or embarrassment in me. When she died, that love in me died also: grief shakes us with ague, but it steadies us with frost also. I remember my mother taking me into the bedroom to see her body. It is said of utter misery that it cannot be remembered – I cannot recall my feelings when I saw her. Only that it seemed as if I were looking at the entire world from a great height. I can still visualise her faintly – her face haunts me still, as if it were a photograph of my own face as a child.

Sir William Wilde, my mother's husband, was an utterly disappointed man. He could never rest – time seemed to him a hateful thing which he felt compelled to master, to wrench into submission like a tiger which threatened his life. For no apparent reason, he would leave the house and walk very quickly down the street: I would run out after him, and see him striding down Westland Row. He would return again five minutes later, with an expression of intense joy upon his face, and retire at once into his library. He was a most untidy and dirty man, given to snorting while holding one finger to his nostril. While at table he would often pick his nails with an old quill pen which he carried in his jacket, and leave the dirt upon the cloth.

When once I complained of this to my mother, she laughed. 'He means no harm, Oscar,' she said, 'leave him be.'

'But how can a doctor be so filthy?'

'He has his own ways, Oscar, and he is a good doctor.'

'But do his patients never complain?' I did not know then that it was for his licentiousness they rebuked him, not his dirtiness. My mother adopted a stern expression, and I fled upstairs.

Sir William was only truly at ease when he travelled to our house in Moytura, where he would spend his days digging among the strange stone and tumuli which in that Western region resemble the outcrop of some terrible extinguished civilisation. Sometimes, reluctantly, he would take me with him on his expeditions: he seemed to me then like an old man who had once wandered with the fairies and wanted to return to their fierce kingdom. We discovered a cross once, an ancient Celtic thing, and he capered around it in delight. We carried it back to the house – I have carried many crosses since then, alas – but Annie, the housekeeper, would not allow us to bring it over the threshold. It was a cursed thing, she said, to move a sacred stone. Sir William always respected the superstitions of the people, and so we took the cross down with us to the shore of Lough Corib. But such was his enthusiasm that, when we left for Dublin, he wrapped it in old cloths and brown paper and took it with us on the train. I passed the whole journey praying that we would not crash. Since that time, parcels have always exercised an odd fascination for me – one always expects something of a sensational nature, and one is always disappointed. In that respect, they resemble the modern novel.

Sir William once took me with him across the water to the island of Aranmore, that wilderness of broken rock with its strange hive-like dwellings. While Sir William rushed on ahead our guide told me that, the year before, one of his children had been taken by the fairies. He had been in bed with his child, but he could not sleep – and then something came close to the window and he heard the high voices of the fairy host. In the morning the child was dead. The implacability of his story, and the cheerful demeanour of the peasant as he told it, impressed me deeply: there is nothing one can do with one's Fate except laugh at it. Of course I was incredulous then but now, in the half-life which I am leading, I am inclined more and more to place my trust in shadowy, supernatural things. The beauty of belief lies in its simplicity – and I have come to understand that life is a simple, a terribly simple, thing.

Sir William was at peace in Moytura because in the city he felt himself to be an object of scorn. He was never able to retain the position to which he was entitled in Dublin society. The rich people who lived near us laughed at him for his peculiar manner and his uncouth dress, just as they laughed secretly at my mother for her somewhat unique appearance. It enraged me to see them do so, but I said nothing. When once I spoke to Willie of it, he remonstrated with me for my absurd pride, as he saw it.

'What is it to you, Hoscar? Keep your nose in your books, if I were you. And then you shan't see them laughing at you also.'

'Who laughs at me?'

23

'Everyone does. And are we going to cry now?'

I fled from him, and I could hear his own laughter as I did so. But I learned by such encounters to control and hide those feelings which might otherwise be injurious to me.

It was a lesson which carried me through my years at Portora, my school, where I was forced to lead a life for which I was not prepared by temperament. I was quite wretched, and in the dormitory at night I would hug myself tight in order to prevent my cries from breaking out. There was a matron there who was kind to me, however: I would come to her in my night-shirt and beg her to take me home. Of course she could not do so, but she comforted me and I would tell her of my mother.

In my first year at Portora, the terrible scandal about Sir William's seduction of a patient was known throughout Ireland. My contemporaries laughed and joked about it, but I was too young to understand. I was bewildered by their laughter, but I turned my bewilderment to scorn and laughed at them. I would lie to my school fellows about my family and my own past. I told them that the Swedish king was my godfather, that we had in Dublin so many servants that I could not count them. I so fancifully blurred the distinction between what was true and what was false that my companions were reduced to silence; even Willie was impressed, and could not bring himself to contradict me.

It was then that I learned the first secret of the imagination: an amusing fantasy has more reality than a commonplace truth. And another secret was revealed to me also: I made them laugh, and then they could not hurt me. Although like all children they found their greatest pleasure in vulgar sarcasm – they called me 'Grey Cow' because of the pallor of my skin – I would draw the sting from that sarcasm by becoming more extravagant than they could possibly have foreseen. I would twist my limbs into the contorted attitudes of the Early Christian martyrs depicted on the windows of the chapel – unfortunately, I seem to be in the same position now – and they were amused. I found the masters there fascinating as caricature, and I would imitate them in a remorseless manner. When in the classroom they adopted expressions which I had parodied earlier, I would be filled with a wild merriment and be forced to stuff a handkerchief in my mouth to prevent myself from laughing out loud. The boys would see and shout, 'You are so wild, Wilde,' and I was known, to masters and pupils alike, as 'that Wilde man from Borneo'. I was not popular, but I was accepted. But these were the sons of Ireland. I learned, too late, that the English can laugh and at the same strike you down, without the least compunction. It is the secret of their success as a nation.

Unlike Willie, who found enlightenment only upon the playing fields, I took a great, indeed an inordinate, interest in my studies. It was in my last years at school that I first discovered Plato and the pre-Socratic philosophers. I trembled with excitement when I sat down to their translation: for me, the joy of my studies lay in the making of connections, in so skilful an organisation of knowledge that, if I wished, I could bring everything within the bright kingdom which opened itself out to me. Intellectual excitement is for me the rarest and most pleasurable kind; to trace the curve of a beautiful thought, to discern the lineaments of an ancient language, and to perceive the living connections between one philosophy and another: these were the joys I first discovered at Portora. Of course the other boys knew nothing of this. I took care to hide my excitement and my knowledge from them. It is a mistake to reveal one's true feelings to the world, for then they are destroyed. I learned the lesson early, did I not?

While the others were composing poems in ugly Latin on 'The Ruins of Paestum' or the 'Cascade of Terri' I was reading the philosophy and the drama of the Athenian people. I read the Bible for recreation merely: it takes a steady course of biblical study in childhood to remove any taint of Christianity from the adult. But there was one phrase, in Proverbs, that revealed to me even then the terrible nature of divinity: 'I also will laugh at your Calamity: I will mock when your fear cometh'. These are the only words of Scripture that seem to me to have an unambiguous meaning. I have ever since thought of God as some spangled, clownish being. His laughter haunts me down the boulevards of this bleak city.

And so by degrees I grew apart from my school-fellows and, in my loneliness, I determined upon fame. By my sixteenth or seventeenth year the pursuit of intellectual clarity and excellence was balanced within me by the overpowering, sweet urge for success. I used to identify myself with every distinguished character whom I discovered in my books. I fell in love with magnificent dreams, and splendours of language. One never outgrows one's early enthusiasms: one merely denies them. And when, in the days of my happiness, I read to my own sons passages

25

from Verne and from Stevenson I often secretly imagined I was the hero of their adventures.

When I was sixteen I discovered Disraeli. I devoured *Vivian Grey* under the bedclothes. I admired his fantastic dress. I loved the melodrama of his life, and the glory of his self-idolatry. When I read that wonderful description of the portrait of Max Rodenstein – a being beautiful both in body and in soul – and how that portrait moved, I could not trust myself to speak. Of course Disraeli is not to be compared with Aeschylus – and I did not do so. The imagination of a boy does not differentiate between sensations, and in Disraeli I discovered the true language of desire in which I might lose myself. The life of the society which was there revealed to me dazzled me, and it was all the brighter since I was at so great a distance from it. But I could not think of it without a terrible sense of the inadequacy of my own position. I decided to remedy it, and I did not care by what method.

17 August 1900

Maurice came this morning, armed with scandals. Joseph was arrested last night on the Boulevard Pasteur: well, if he travels to the suburbs he deserves to be arrested. Joseph is a sweet boy: he insists that I call him Mary, although I told him that the character of a virgin is always more suspect than that of a carpenter. A woman hanged herself last night in the Boulevard Sébastopol, right next to the Petits Agneaux – whether in protest against the displays in their front windows, it is impossible yet to determine. Then Maurice asked me for my own news.

'Did I tell you about my cousin Lionel?'

'No. Because you have no cousin Lionel.'

'Well, Lionel wished to become a writer. I told him that only thoroughly good people ever become writers, but he was quite insistent. He wrote back to me: What about Hall Caine?'

'Oscar, you are talking nonsense, as usual.'

'I replied, Who is Hall Caine? Never trust anyone who sounds like a Scottish residence. But Lionel was adamant. Only yesterday he sent me the first line of his novel. Do you wish to hear it?'

'If it is short.'

'It goes – "Those are excellent apricots, are they not?" I have written to tell him that he should go on; I long to hear the answer. I know so little about apricots. No, Maurice, I am afraid I have very little news: I am dying and, what is more, I have no cigarettes.'

Maurice left me two or three 'weeds', as he calls them in his strange English, before he retired to the relative safety of the streets. I cannot exist without cigarettes: the first, and I think the most awful, experience of prison life came when I was denied them. The secret of my identity disappeared at once: like God, my face should always be seen behind clouds. Now, whenever I think of that terrible period, I feel some absurd need to light one. I smoke continually, of course. Cigarettes are the torches of self-consciousness, and under their influence I can withdraw from the world into a sphere of private sensation. I lie upon my bed, and watch the fumes curl towards the ceiling. It is the only entertainment which my bed provides.

I do not sleep in it, at least not in the manner which doctors prescribe. My nerves may be exhausted, but they have a strange facility for reminding me of their presence My little Jewish doctor tells me that I suffer from neurasthenia I told him that only advanced people suffer from that particular complaint, at least according to Ouida, and that I was quite happy to accept his diagnosis. Indeed, I was flattered to be thought worthy of it.

I have always suffered from nervous disabilities. In earlier years I grew pale and sick with asthma, and as I grew older I often lay prostrate with various complaints which cleverly anticipated the crises of my life. The body has a strange consciousness of its own and, when I was surrounded by renters or by creditors, or when I could not work upon my plays, it would plunge me into disorder. The body can detect misery and disaster even before the spirit feels them. This is no doubt the message which Mr Darwin has left us: it only waits to be discovered within the medieval mysteries of his prose. I am tired now: I must rest.

18 August 1900

I was speaking of my childhood, was I not? I believe it was even then that my fate was measured out, although only by chance was this revealed to me. Frank Houlihan, who worked for my father at Moytura, took me, on one holiday from school, to an old peasant woman who had a reputation in the neighbourhood for the telling of men's fortunes. He had told me of her often, and I felt a strange desire to see her. I hoped, I think, that she would recognise in me what I had already discovered in myself.

She was a withered thing, wearing the red dress common to the women of that region. She took my hand – large, even then, and grey – and surveyed it in a somewhat scornful manner. But then she stroked my arm, and told me that my fate was to be both magnificent and terrible, that my name, Oscar, famous in the annals of Irish history, would sit upon me – she said – as a dream of far-off things continues into the day.

Frank and I travelled back in the cart in silence. I received then a sense of fate which has never left me. I knew, from my reading at Portora, that the point of all tragedy is the heedlessness of the tragic hero: even when he has seen the curse, he runs towards it willingly. Of course I had no one to weave beautiful songs out of my destiny – but, then, I have always been my own chorus.

I have never spoken about my childhood before, even to those who have known me and shared my sorrows, because it bears witness to a shame not my own. When I lay like a wounded animal in my mother's house, on bail between my trials, she came to me weeping and told me that she held herself responsible for my fate, and that the punishment I was suffering was for her own sin: that I was not Sir William's child. I am illegitimate. I do not wonder why I could not speak Sir William's name without sighing, and why I do not in the least resemble him. I see now why in Merrion Square I seemed always to be the one set apart, and why my mother did her best to shield me from the world, in case I had inherited the sensual disposition with which she had conceived me.

My mother, on that fateful evening, told me that my father was an Irish poet and patriot who had died many years before; his name was Smith O'Brien. She told me that he used to visit us when she took me to the little farmhouse which we owned in the vale of Glencree – I had quite forgotten that farmhouse. But I can recall dimly a quiet man who would come and play with me, let me win at childish games and press a coin into my hand. His name is not unknown to me – he was one of those who suffered terribly for Ireland's sake and, when I recall the dignity he seemed to possess when I knew him as a child, I know also that it is the dignity of one who has failed.

As my mother told me of those days, she wept; and, indeed, I pitied her rather than myself. She had hidden her sorrow and, when we conceal the past, like a fox beneath a cloak, it injures us. Only in my own tragedy had she the strength to come to me and, in short, quiet words, tell me of her dishonour that bound her to my own. In her guilt, she had shut out the sun all those years; she had sat in darkness.

And although I felt nothing then – so many blows had been rained upon me that I was numb to further suffering – now it helps me to understand. The workings of the personality are mysterious to me and yet the dark thread which runs through my life can, I think, be detected in my strange beginning. The illegitimate are forced to create themselves, to stand upright even when the whirlwind engulfs them. I know now, also, why I longed for praise and for recognition even as I knew that fame and applause were empty things. I have come to understand why I found myself employing conventional values only to mock at them or turn them into parody; why I took refuge in hard, nerve-destroying work, and in that mist of words which clings about me always. My mother's confession confirmed that I, too, ranked among the outcasts – but I am not sure that murmurings of my lot had not always reached me in my private ear.

21 August 1900

In 1871 I entered Trinity College, Dublin. I was, I believe, seventeen but already I felt like an eagle who has been forced to find rest among sparrows. It was an extension of school merely, in which discontent at my position was piled upon the aimlessness and weariness which I always suffer when I am not surrounded by laughter and by brightly coloured companions. Even as a boy, I had passed it with a shudder. It seemed to me then to resemble some prison, although I was to discover later that the comparison was not an exact one.

My tutor there, Mahaffy, spoke to me of Greek things, but not without a few delicate elisions. 'Read Plato for his conversation,' he would announce to me. 'Read Peacock for his philosophy, if you must, but read Plato in order to discover how to turn speech into drama and conversation into an art.' And so at night I would read the *Phaedo* in a loud voice. I translated Aristophanes and made him sound like Swinburne. I read Swinburne, and thought it farcical. I did not care then for many of the authors whom we were compelled to study. Virgil's chilly, sententious verses and the absurd lucubrations of Ovid bored me; I detested the braggadocio of Cicero and the earnest dullness of Caesar. I turned instead to the sonorous African Latin of Apuleius and to the dry, hard little sentences of Tertullian writing and preaching when Elogabolus was at work. But I cared above all for Petronius, whose *Satyricon* woke in me an appreciation of new sensations. I did not wish to experience them: it was enough to know that they existed.

Dublin seemed to me to be even more decayed and helpless. My mother was drinking, and attempted to hide the fact by retiring to her room in the early afternoon. Sir William was making himself ill with overwork and refused to acknowledge the extent of my mother's weakness. He wanted me to remain at Trinity, and eventually take up a position there – I would even now have been lecturing on the Eumenides, instead of being pursued by them – but I declined absolutely. I pitied Sir William, as one pities those for whom life has become a snare, but I had no intention of inviting a fate similar to his own.

And so you can imagine my joy when, after three years, I was awarded the demyship and journeyed to Oxford. It came as a revelation to me: the journey was from the medieval pieties of my native soil to the open thought of Hellenism. It was my own renaissance. In those unfamiliar surroundings I felt immediately at ease. Touched by the light of that university I came to life although, at first, it was of a fitful and halting kind. I was eager for friendship then, rather than learning, and in my early months I found it where I could. They were decent, good chaps at Magdalen and with certain of them I would laugh and talk late into the night.

'And what do you want to do, Oscar?' one of them might say.

'To do? I don't want to do anything. I want to *be* everything.'

'You do talk rot, sometimes.'

'Actually, I would like to be Pope.'

'But you pretend to be so wicked, Oscar.'

'Then I would excommunicate myself at once.'

'No, you will become a schoolmaster. I see it in your face.'

'My face is my most deceptive feature. My fate, dear boy, is written on my hand.'

'That is why it is so limp, I suppose.'

And yet sometimes in these happy hours the flat meadows around Magdalen inspired in me feelings of the deepest melancholy, as if my first ambitious hopes might themselves spread out and disappear into the damp landscape which surrounded me. I had what Ruskin called 'the restlessness of the dreaming mind'; he considered it a virtue, but then I was bewildered by it.

I was, I believe now, treading that treacherous path which every artist must take before he reaches his own kingdom. I had no ideals and no opinions, I was tired of the learning that I could too quickly master, desirous of fame and yet unsure how to claim it, desiring love also and yet frightened to find it – since, in truth, I did not know in what shadows it might be hiding. I worked hard, although I concealed the fact from my contemporaries, because it seemed then that through work only could I assert the powers of personality which I knew existed in me. But I knew too many theories to believe in one absolutely – I disbelieved in everything, including myself. I was ambitious, but to no particular end.

For it was my fate to attain the self-consciousness of an artist at a time when values of all kind had been thrown into doubt. I was later to believe that I might find art and the values of art in the creation of my own personality and that, like Zeus and Athene all at once, I might emerge more powerful from my own head. But at Oxford I was of an age when, with no guiding instinct of my own except ambition, I sought for authority where I could.

The Roman Church in those years entranced me with the poetry of its ritual and the power of its liturgy. I would read Thomas à Kempis and, dazzled by his sonorous low tone, would imagine myself an anchorite dwelling in silence and in prayer. The Church seemed to be a supreme example of the triumph of aesthetics over morality, evoking strange rituals and sorrowful renunciations. I felt a secret pleasure in renouncing my own sins – especially those which I had not committed.

But the Roman faith could not satisfy me. I believed that, just as certain extraordinary chemicals can only be discerned when they are bathed in a particular solution, if I were immersed in the atmosphere of fine thoughts and fine words I, too, might stand revealed. And I sought for all those who might assist me, whose personalities were so powerful that in their presence I might acquire an especial note of my own.

It was to John Ruskin that I went first, ready like the sinner of Decapolis to touch his robe and feel the power enter into me. I had searched for his books in Dublin and found in them a strength of conviction which, in my own incapacity, touched me deeply, and I remember my awe on seeing him enter the lecture theatre for the first time. He entered bearing a plate – a breakfast plate, I believe – and, without waiting for us to settle, began to speak of the pink roses drawn upon it and the band of green traced around its edge. He asked us, as an impanelled jury, to decide upon the question of the plate. Was it well done, as the expression of a virtuous craftsman, or was it badly done, the product of a vicious one? He held it up and no one spoke: indeed, his too felicitous expressions seemed to derive from some distant epoch, and there were those who laughed secretly. But then he continued as if he had asked no question at all. He talked about his striding through London – yes, striding was the word and how well it suited the image I had formed of him – and his disgust at the friezes and brackets which mutilated the exterior fronts of grocers and hosiers. He wished to tear them off, he said, and, as he spoke, he snatched at the air.

After his lecture, he asked for help with building his road to Ferry Hinksey, and I volunteered at once. It was not out of a desire to enter into physical labour of any sort – one should only engage in those activities where one can become preeminent –but simply in order that I might meet him. I knew that, if I could spend some hours with him, I could fortify my own character by imitation. The road itself was not a success: I believe it stopped somewhere in the middle of a field. Indeed, I learned so much about the body of man under socialism that afterwards I cared only to write about the soul.

Ruskin would give tea in his rooms to those of us who worked on the unfortunate project. We would sit in a circle and listen merely – one had only to agree, and one became a pupil. There was, I believe, something of the bully in him and he could give the most intellectual inquiry an air of menace. There was no general conversation. On one occasion he stared at me in the middle of one of his more irridescent monologues – 'And tell us, Mr Wilde, your opinion of domestic implements.' I described at some length the customary kitchen tools of Galway – I have always believed, in moments of uncertainty, in saying the first thing that occurs to me, hoping that it will have the enchantment of all first things –and he seemed to be pleased with my answer. 'The Celts,' he said, 'protect their land with beauty.' I thought that a wonderful sentence, and I believe I used it on later occasions.

Ruskin was a familiar sight in Oxford, walking with his blue frock-coat and blue cravat in even the most uncertain weather, half-frowning and half-pleased when he was recognised by those whom he passed. He had a theatrical aspect to his character which enlivened the dramatic vein within my own temperament. Sometimes he would allow me to walk with him, and talk of Gothic things – I was the Mrs Siddons to his Irving. I must pause – Agnes has called me to the telephone. She is so frightened of the instrument that, judging by her tone, I might be going to the scaffold.

'Oui, Monsieur Melmoth qui parle. Oh it's you, my dear.' I knew at once that the terrible hissing sound was not that of the telephone: it was merely Charles Ricketts, who for some reason always giggles when he hears my voice. 'Well, Charles, I am waiting.'

'Can you hear me, Oscar?'

'Of course I can hear you.' I intensely dislike the telephone. It is suitable only for really intimate conversations.

'I am giving a party, Oscar.'

34

'Oui.'

'Just for a few old flames.'

'Well, you will have to hire the Albert Hall then, dear.'

'Oh don't, Oscar, you are frightful.'

'Mais oui.' More giggles.

'Actually, I was thinking of using the upstair room in the Café Julien. You like it there, don't you?'

'I like it there immensely. I shall wear my tiara, deuxième classe.'

'You will come, won't you, Oscar? Everyone is dying to meet you.'

'So am I.'

'Well, that's settled then. How are you, dear Oscar?'

'I am perfectly well, my dear, thank you. At the moment I am writing a most imaginative account of my youth.'

'I shall send him an invitation also.'

'That is most kind of you, Charles. He loves crowds.'

'And Oscar – '

'Yes?'

'Do take care of yourself.'

'A bientôt, dear.'

22 August 1900

Now, where was I? Ah, yes. But if at Oxford I learned from Ruskin the integrity of individual perception, it was from Walter Pater that I learned the poetry of feeling. I attended his lectures on Plato and Platonism and the beauty of his low, chaste 'intonation trainante' remains with me still. I did not meet him until my final year; he had admired some slight article which I had written about the Grosvenor Gallery, and he invited me to tea. What a strange contrast the man presented: in feature a Boer farmer, in manner a vestal virgin. His was an essentially feminine temperament which was trapped inside quite the wrong body. His rooms would have been suitable for St Cyril or St Bernard – there was a sixteenth-century Pietà on one wall, otherwise completely bare, and Baskerville editions of the classics on his shelves – and indeed there is more true piety in Pater's accounts of the Greek myths than in the whole of Newman.

At that first meeting, I felt that my physical presence caused him a certain unease – I am aware of that with others, also, who draw back when they see me. I once remarked to Reggie Turner that I had the figure of Nero; Reggie, who has a tongue of fire, replied, 'But made out of suet, Oscar.' Well, Pater retired to a safe distance in the event of my toppling over. We saw much of each other after that, but there was always a curious nervousness about our meetings. I remember once, in a moment of threnody when we were discussing the *Symposium*, inadvertently placing my hand upon his arm and he started as though I had seared him with a brand. It was a moment of supreme discomfort for both of us.

He would finger a tortoise-shell paper knife as he spoke, continually rubbing it up and down his moustache and then carefully replacing it on the table in front of him. He was capable of the most extraordinary enthusiasms, and then his Sibylline whisper would change to a louder note. Ruskin, I think, despised him but that did not prevent him from speaking of Ruskin with great reverence. Poor Pater, I felt – and still feel – for him an infinite pity mixed with an infinite gratitude. 'I want,' he told me once, 'to lift the veil of the blindfold – to see life in its exact relations.' I do not believe he ever did. He was too retiring and innocent a man to understand that life cannot be seen. It can only be suffered.

But I owe Pater everything: just as I learnt in his prose the secrets of his bashful art, so it was through his eyes that I first saw myself as an artist. In his delicate praise of my work, he gave me the gift of self-awareness and it was he who suggested the direction I was later to follow: he urged me to forsake the revelations of poetry for the intimations of prose. Poetry, he said, was the higher art; but prose was the more difficult.

And indeed my own poetry was perhaps too facile. I worked swiftly, under the direct impress of those modes which most fascinated me. I saw everything as words, for in words could I hide from myself. Without them I stumbled blindly. I addressed myself to the gods because I did not wish to see that which was closer to hand. It seems to me now that many of my poems were written to young men but, since I called them by Greek or Roman names, neither I nor they knew anything whatever about it. I carried the shield of the true poet everywhere with me, not understanding then that a shield can crush one also.

In my last year I won the Newdigate Prize for an elegy on Ravenna. I was taken in procession like a fatted calf to the Sheldonian, where I recited the more violet passages of that terribly flawed poem. It was a wonderful moment, and I borrowed for the occasion some of the techniques which I had seen employed with great effect at the Brompton Oratory. It was my first taste of success as an artist, but one that led me fatally to believe that success would always surround me.

When the poem was published in volume form, I suffered agonies of conscience. There is something both magnificent and terrible about one's first book – it goes out into the world unwillingly because it takes so much of its creator with it also, and the creator always wishes to call it home. I wrote the poem in a deliberately conventional manner and yet, by wearing the mask of my own age, I realise that I could express quite directly my own feelings. Although in their natural state they were quite deficient in form, I was able in my verse to marshall them in perfect order. I found myself by borrowing another's voice. And I was applauded for it: here we have the wonderful beginnings of an artist, do we not, touched only lightly by the shadow of later tragedy?

23 August 1900

But if at Oxford I felt as if I were experiencing the joys of a renaissance, I also knew that in turn I must attempt to bury my own recent past. I learned to lose, by stealth, the remnants of an Irish accent just as I discarded checks and bowlers for the stripes and variegated neckties of modern life.

It has been said that I 'posed' in those days – it is an absurd charge. Those who are aware of their genius, even in childhood, are quite conscious of the disparity between themselves and others. They do not 'pose', they merely draw their own conclusions. But the disparity between what they know themselves to be and that coventional demeanour which the world forces them to adopt – that requires thought to resolve. And so I essayed several personalities, in order to find one which was closest to my own. I dressed for effect, I admit it, but the only person I wished to affect was myself.

The English have no sense of occasion in such matters and I was sometimes ridiculed. I was not, in the jargon of that period, an 'A.1 fellow', a 'top-notcher', and, as a result, I was never on terms of intimacy with my contemporaries. There were exceptions, of course – indeed, exceptions rule English social life.

Frank Miles, the painter, was my greatest friend at Oxford. Alas, he died in a private asylum in Ongar. I visited him there, just before his death; he had a small room and as I entered, under the watchful eye of an attendant, he bowed low in mock homage to me. 'Ah, I see they have let you out too, Oscar?' In his conversation he had the strange clarity of the possessed, and I felt helpless before it, like an infant before the thunder. He slapped me on the back, and roared with laughter: 'Oscar,' he said, 'you must learn to carry a hazelwood stick, to ward off the damned.' After some minutes of this painful banter, he turned his face to the wall and would not look at me. 'Remember,' he kept on repeating, 'the dog it was that died. The dog it was that died.' In my bewilderment, I looked at the attendant, who winked at me and showed me to the door. I was about to leave when Frank rushed over to a small desk, upon which were a series of drawings. He handed me one of them: 'Here is your own flower, Oscar. The flower of forgetting.' My own name had been traced out in a series of concentric circles, in green and scarlet ink, so that the whole composition seemed to be of some monstrous blossom in which the petals were still unfolding. I hurried from that wretched place as from ground where blood has been shed, and, as soon as I left the asylum, I threw the thing away. Lord Ronald Gower, who is the younger son of the Duke of Sutherland, and with whom I was once on terms of the closest intimacy, told me that Frank believed that I had fashioned his personality and then allowed it to fall into ruins. It is an absurd charge.

Frank was a wild, agreeable boy at Oxford – I believe that I discerned in him even then the scarlet specks of madness and I have always been interested in the daemonic qualities of others. But I was attracted to Frank, also, because he was part of that Society which I had glimpsed in my lonely reading; through Lord Ronald Gower, he knew the Duchess of Westminster, and those others of wealth and position who were to me fabulous beings. For the first time I had met someone of my own age who exercised a fascination over me, and from whom I could learn.

Indeed Frank actively encouraged the growth of my personality. He encouraged me in any excess of high spirits, so that I felt myself propelled ever faster towards the character which beckoned to me – alas, that character was myself. I learned from Frank also the slight drawl which I affected for a few years, and from him also the rhythms of that destructive wit which I found so attractive.

He would come every morning to my rooms in Magdalen, and examine with ever-renewed satisfaction the figures which he had painted upon the doors. 'You know, Oscar,' he said on one occasion, 'I think I might have to fill this wall here with something in yellow.'

'I detest yellow, Frank, it looks so calculating.'

'Green, then?'

'Green is unnatural. Do leave the walls alone, Frank, they have been quite happy without you.'

He would wander around my rooms in a wilful manner, picking up objects and scrutinising them carefully. 'Really, Oscar, you must lose this ash-tray. It is hideous, and you hardly ever smoke.'

'I am learning to, by trial and error. But you are right about the ash-tray. I shall replace it at once.'

'And what do you intend doing about this etching of Raphael's Madonna? I know you are turning Roman, but Raphael is really *de trop*. Do you know nothing about art?'

'It is not a question of art, Frank. I have been trying to imitate the Madonna's expression. It is so useful at tutorials.' I pretended to be unmoved, but I removed the etching that evening. I told Frank that it had been assumed into heaven.

'You assume too much,' he replied.

We both laughed; in those days we assailed each other with extravagant phrases, and then carefully examined them. 'No, Oscar,' Frank would tell me, 'don't say, "It is a terrible thing that . . ." That sounds like an Irish expression. Simply say, "It is terrible that . . ."' He was immensely helpful to me.

We were inseparable then and, if I say that we loved each other, I do not intend it in the Uranian fashion. Even on our holidays, when we shared a bed together, we did not indulge in the practices of schoolboys. There was romance between us, but it was the romance of young men who find that their ambitions coincide. Frank was the Painter and I was the Poet: with these gilded words we concealed the hunger for fame that spurred us forward. But I committed the error of which all great artists are guilty – I believed that the stirrings of my own heart had the wonderful impersonality of genius, and that in the exploration of my own character I might find new subjects for poetry and new forms of art. I know now that I was wrong, but I went to London armed with that fantasy – for I had come to conquer.

24 August 1900

When I arrived in London from Oxford, it seemed to me that I was leaving Athens in order to find Rome. And just as Caesar Augustus celebrated a new century some years in advance of its proper date, so in London the gods of a new age had already arrived on swift feet. The city then was in a ferment. Ugly buildings were torn down and uglier ones raised in their place, and the rookeries which are London's only contribution to the Romantic movement were demolished for the sake of a few unnecessary roads. It was said that an old man had been buried in the foundations of New Oxford Street – one can only hope it was the architect.

From the first faint stirrings of dawn, when the carts clattered towards Covent Garden with their jade-coloured vegetables, to the shouts and catcalls at the dead of night, the city did not rest. And when by the Thames, in the early evening, the rows of electric lights stood out against the sky, I believed that I had never seen anything so beautiful. It was, like Seager's Gin, the spirit of today and of tomorrow.

But I tired easily of the brightness and sought instead the shadows which surround it. I took a nervous delight in walking through narrow courts and alleys, among men and women of evil aspect. In these ancient streets off the main thoroughfares, I saw squalor and shame but to me they were picturesque only: I was not to discover their real secrets until later. Here ragged boys, without shoes or stockings, sold newspapers or turned cartwheels for a penny; here also young children would stand in silence around Italian organs, and then be called by strange voices into the public houses where I dared not follow.

But, if I shrank back from a life I could not understand, I could at least experience it in my imagination. The world of the theatres and the music halls was my principal delight. I would go alone and sit – not with the inhabitants of the Hackney villas in the stalls but with the common people in the pit. I would visit the Alhambra and watch with fascination Arthur Roberts, who could transform London life into a fantasy worthy of Otway's harsh laughter or Goya's grotesques. When the dusty orchestra struck up a tune and Roberts began to sing, in his odd, cracked voice, 'Will you stand me a cab fare, ducky, I'm feeling so awfully queer,' the pit roared with laughter. How I envied him his position on that stage. At the end of each performance I would feel a strange elation, and I would wander out with the crowd whose faces seemed bright and powerful under the glare of the gas lamps.

In my youthful imagination I saw London as a vast furnace which might maim or destroy all those that it touched, but which also created light and heat. It was as if all the powers of the earth had been concentrated on this spot, and my personality was immeasurably enriched by it. Since those days, I have always been an inhabitant of cities: I could not have known then that I was one day to become a monument to the diseases of urban civilisation. In London I thought to understand every form of human activity but, instead, I tasted every aspect of human corruption.

If I sought anonymity in my wanderings, I also feared it. Frank Miles and I took rooms together near the river, behind the Strand where the noise of the cabs and the omnibuses was positively Wagnerian. But nothing could then have discouraged us, for we had come to London in the belief that it would be a continuation of the painted pageant of our days at Oxford. We sought fame and, in our innocence, found notoriety instead.

Charmed by Frank's skills as a painter almost as much as they were impressed by his social connections, and amused by my ability to flatter without being indiscreet, a succession of beautiful women would come to take tea with us at Thames House. In those days women controlled society, as they have done in all the really civilised periods. The men were too busy, or too dull, to play a major part in the social life which we entered then for the first time. We conquered by day and celebrated our triumphs at night – rather cheaply, I think, in the Florence.

I knew in those days more women than I was ever to know again. The Duchess of Westminster and the Duchess of Beaufort came, followed almost too quickly by Lily Langtry and Ellen Terry. Frank painted them and I amused them. I have always, in the modern phrase, 'got on' with women: I understand them. But in those days I worshipped them also because, with the subtle arts of their sex, they had learned how to dominate life. I can remember walking down the Strand with Lily one evening, when the cab-drivers hailed her, and the people turned around to look back at her. I basked in her glory but even then I considered how much more interesting it would be if it were happening to me.

I knew from the beginning, of course, that I would never possess the absurd gravitas of the English gentleman, who employs scorn when he has nothing to say and adopts an air of preoccupation when he has nothing whatever to think about. And so I accompanied those women who had conquered society with their wonderful personalities, and I learned from them. They were the great artists of my period and, in my dramas, I paid them the compliment of making them far more intelligent and terrible than the men – like all artists, after all, they are far less rational.

And so I became the confidant of those women who were interested in their husbands, whom they rarely saw, and bored by their lovers, who always saw them. I would go with Lady Dudley to her dressmaker, and discovered from her the secret of speaking to a tailor: always lower one's voice. As a result I became something of an expert on women's fashions – these were the days when I favoured green and yellow rather than purple and gold. I would go to Lady Sebright's wonderful house in Lowndes Square where we would discuss the promise, if any, of that evening's dinner party. We would devise the seating plan together as if it were another Peninsular War. I had learned by now how to amuse her – I would make fun of those whom she professed to like, and talk extremely seriously about those whom she found ridiculous.

When Helen Modjeska was rehearsing *La Dame aux Camélias* at the little Court theatre in Sloane Square, she asked me to visit her there. Frank had just completed a peculiarly flattering portrait of her, and I believe she wanted to be near anyone who had seen it. When I arrived, the theatre was empty and, in semi-darkness, the flats were drawn into position and the stage hands shouted to each other above the hammering and the sawing. Then there was silence. La Modjeska came onto the stage. In that fiery moment, which has always been a source of wonder to me, she ceased to be the person whom I knew; when she walked from the dusky recesses of the wings and moved in to the glare of the electric lamps, she was transformed. I had a vision then which I scarcely understood, for it was a vision of the world.

44

It seemed natural in those days that everyone should be in London and so, at dinners or at large gatherings, one met the people who either controlled or entertained society – although it was sometimes difficult to distinguish between them. I did not view such proceedings with complete seriousness, and I cannot say that I was impressed, personally, even by those whose work I admired. I adored Meredith as a novelist, for example – he is one of the few cases in recent literature of a writer whose poetry is more comprehensible than his prose, so of course I preferred his prose – but as a man he was a severe disappointment. He had the melancholy expression of a verger who has been told that there will be no more services today. I met Swinburne – once only, but I believe that was the common experience. He seemed to me a shy, awkward fellow. Often he drew his hand across his face, as if trying to shield his eyes from the world. Frank and I would imitate him, when we returned laughing to Thames House, but now I look upon him with great pity. I remember remarking, at the time, that he was forced to live in Putney, and was as a consequence contributing only to the *Nineteenth Century*. But I see now that his tragedy was similar to my own: he suddenly lost his genius, and with it his ability to dominate his own life. I should have seen that, and loved him for it.

I had a great aversion to Matthew Arnold. I sat opposite to him, dining at Lord Wharncliffe's, I think, and he had the satisfied countenance of a man who has never succeeded in boring himself. He was a vain, elongated creature who would have bent forward to see his own reflection in a puddle. We were discussing the new French dramatists: he sounded like a Methodist preacher advising against the use of crematoria. I believe that he wanted to fill the theatres of the West End with the middle-classes, and so set an example to the world. I disagreed, naturally, but of course he paid no attention to me.

And indeed it is possible that I was not impressed by the great and the distinguished simply because they were not impressed by me. I was about to publish a volume of poems and I was completing my first play, *Vera*, but my literary work was considered to be of no importance. Even after we had moved to Chelsea, our callers were women principally – and they were interested only in those poems which were addressed to themselves. My reputation, such as it was, had nothing whatever to do with my serious work and so, out of the bitter gaiety which springs from the consciousness of failure, I made fun of myself as well as of others. I became an aesthete, but neither Gilbert nor Sullivan could have mocked me as much as I mocked myself.

Once I read an extract from *Vera* to Lily, but she was not a success as an audience. She asked for more tea in the middle of a beautiful speech, and walked distractedly around the room, fingering the photographs of herself, while I wept over a passage of more than usual beauty. When Lily was not the centre of attention, she had no sense of occasion. She once brought to my rooms an enormous stuffed peacock, popularly assumed to have been shot by the Earl of Warwick. The death of such a bird, she declared, was supposed to bring misfortune. 'But then,' she said, 'some people believe anything at all.' I looked at her with horror, and threw the peacock out of the window, much to the surprise of passing pedestrians. It was probably the only time in our friendship that Lily and I quite understood each other. But she was right, I now believe, to ignore *Vera*: it was suitable only for the ears of the deaf. I cannot think of that play without embarrassment. There was poetry in it, but unfortunately none of it was my own. One can forgive Shakespeare anything, except one's own bad lines.

But nevertheless it was a source of bitter disappointment to me, in those first years in London, that other artists had no confidence in my own talent. I had thought to come to London and announce myself, but I could find no one to listen. If I had shown them holes in my hands, and a wound in my side, they would have paid just as little attention. I had imagined, also, that there was a camaraderie among artists which transcended the trivial obligations of social life – of course, none whatever existed. Whistler lived opposite us in Chelsea; he was a frequent visitor, but he came only so that he could talk about himself in different company. The only way to silence him was to be more extravagant than he was – when he had paused for breath. I think I succeeded too well; he never forgave me the fact that, while people smiled at his remarks, they laughed at my own. His was the failure of the American temperament: he took himself too seriously, and as a result no one else took him seriously at all. There was a terrible rage beneath even the most extravagant flourishes of his temperament: as an Irishman, I understand that. Poor Jimmy – and now he is about to be enshrined among the Immortals. He will never leave them in peace.

46

25 August 1900

I woke too late this morning to do any proper work. I write only in the mornings – the early light flatters the imagination, just as the evening light flatters the complexion. This journal is, in any event, quite exhausting my powers of invention – having written about London yesterday morning, I was compelled to dream about it all last night.

I was trapped in some flat, phantasmasgoric nightmare. I was standing in Leicester Square, but the ground was curiously paved. The electric lights which had once so entranced me by the Thames seemed harsh and monstrously large: they flickered above the square and all at once I felt myself jostled by a crowd of men and women in ugly, bright clothes. I looked up, and I saw that remarkable advertisement for the Alexandra dentifrice – but the Princess moved and spoke to me. It was quite horrid, and rather frightening, as if a chromolithograph had acquired the powers of motion. I shall at once report the incident to the Society for Psychical Research.

27 August 1900

You can do two things with the English – you can shock them, or you can amuse them. You can never reason with them, at least if the editorials in *The Times* are anything to go by. And so, where Pater had murmured and Ruskin had denounced, I would surprise. They had in sober words argued that the values of art and the imagination were not to be divorced from the practice of life, but it was left to me to become the first convincing demonstration of that truth. I entered my aesthetic phase. I did not walk down Piccadilly with a lily in my hand – I tried not to walk anywhere in those days – but I fashioned a world in which such things became possible. I dressed in either an eighteenth- or a twentieth-century fashion – the glory that had passed or the splendour yet to come, I am not sure which – but I made a definite point of having no connection with my own century. I was astonishing: like Pears Soap, there was no substitute. To my friends I was Stupor Mundi, to my enemies the Anti-Christ.

And indeed I actively desired to stand apart. If I could not yet do so in my writing, I would turn my genius to personal account. Now, in my ruin, there seems to me to be something of melancholy about those who wish to stand above others. It is both offensive and yet pitiable, ironic but also touching: it is the cry of the child for attention and the roar of the beast in pain. But I possessed a sense of myself which the world did not share and so, in my vanity, I resisted the blandishments of the world's conventions. My mother, who had moved to London after Sir William's death, wanted me to follow my brother's example and do journalistic work of a literary nature. I shrank from the prospect: if one touches pitch, of course one is defiled. I disliked the literary authorities and they disliked me. I mocked their values, and they in turn laughed at me. Indeed my personality has

48

always been a problem to others: just as, in later years, my work was to be the object of general bewilderment.

For in those first brilliant years in London, when I had found no genuine or permanent expression outside myself, I shrank from some earnestness in my character and took on the multi-coloured garb of the clown. It seems to me now that I took life too seriously to be able to speak of it without embarrassment. Pliny advised his closest friend to seek in literature deliverance from mortality, advice which I understood perfectly. I was wounded and afraid of life, and so I fled with panting breath and bleeding feet to Art and Beauty, in whose temples I might find sanctuary. Here I concealed myself from the world in the mask of the dandy, when with fatal fluency I pronounced the doctrines of Aestheticism.

So afraid was I of the formlessness of life – it bore the marks of the Chaos from which it sprang, like striations in a wonderful jewel – that I took it with both hands and fashioned it into stories and epigrams, just as later I was to change it into the shape of clever drama. I turned conversation into an art, and my personality into a symbol; with these I braved the emptiness and darkness which threatened to engulf me, that emptiness and darkness which are now my constant companions: how strange it is that one should, in the end, suffer the fate which one most fears.

Naturally, the reasons for my conduct were never understood, even by those who were closest to me; to my enemies, and even to my friends, I was an amiable fool. They never discerned my values, and so it was assumed that I had none. And, in truth, my ideas were often more dignified than myself. And yet they mocked me also because my utter want of seriousness represented a terrible threat to all their values. I was a Nihilist of the imagination, in revolt against my period – although I could hardly be accused of shedding blood, I used the weapons which were closest to hand, for they were those which my own class had fashioned for me.

I was reading Balzac then, and I can still recall the chilling interview of the criminal Vautrin with Lucien de Rubempré, when he saves Lucien from an impulsive suicide by instructing him in the invisible laws of society; by persuading Lucien, the poor poet impelled forward by that curious mixture of anger and ambition which I knew so well, that he could work those laws to his own benefit. 'There are no longer any laws', he whispers to him with the ineffable sweetness of true evil, 'merely conventions: nothing but form.' I was, at that moment I read these terrible sentences, like the ancient king who reads upon a wall the shining letters of his own destiny, although I hardly needed a prophet to decipher them. What had before been an instinct with me became a principle. It completed the first stage of my education which, like any real education, had been conducted by means of a dialogue with myself. Everything seemed to me to be like its own parody – I do not speak of society, for that was its only truly remarkable attribute. But I believed then that almost all the methods and conventions of art and life found their highest expression in parody. I have made that clear in all my work, just as I announced it in my dress and in my behaviour.

It was for this reason that it pleased me somewhat when I became an object of wonder or of ridicule. The fact that a gilded mask was taken for the human face confirmed and strengthened the laws of my own being. It was for that reason, also, that I agreed to go to America in order to lecture upon aesthetics. There I could, in stern conditions resembling those of a laboratory, live up to my own drama.

28 August 1900

Hugo Stern positively bumped into me in the Rue des Beaux Arts yesterday evening: he is German in everything except his conversation, which is Greek.

'Oscar, dear,' he said to me, 'we are celebrating the feast of St Zephyrinus. Do come and join us.'

'You are a day late,' I told him, 'but perhaps the Pope will not hear of it immediately.'

And so I accompanied him to the Kalisaya. It was not a successful occasion. Two young Americans joined us. They insisted that they had been thrown out of Harvard for immoral conduct. I told them that it was immoral to go there in the first place. Then they bought me an absinthe: Americans always buy drinks when they are shocked. They both had the horrid habit of calling each other 'she' and eventually, when they had vine leaves in their hair, they insisted on extending the same courtesy to me.

'She's a very famous woman,' one of them said to the other. I was quite disgusted: to have suffered all I have suffered, to have endured the obloquy of the civilised world, and then to end up as the literary equivalent of Boadicea – well, it is ridiculous.

After I had left the bar with my dignity unimpaired, my fiacre was involved in an awful accident. We were turning into the Rue Bonaparte when the cab lurched into a horse-and-cart, and I was propelled forward banging my head against the low wooden rail. My lip was cut almost in two, and I shed as much blood as a martyr, but a most curious thing happened which I still cannot explain. I laughed. I laughed out loud. For no reason I laughed at my own injury.

29 August 1900

I had heard of America, unfortunately, before it had heard of me. Helen Modjeska once told me that, when she was playing the part of a consumptive in a more than usually exotic Western town, the audience sent round bottles of patent medicine after the performance. I knew at once that it was my duty to visit a people who had so much faith in the powers of art. One is always being told that they are a young nation, but they remain young only because they are rediscovered annually by Europeans. Even English novelists go there now to lecture; unfortunately, most of them come back.

When I was asked by D'Oyly Carte to go myself, in order to boost his production of *Patience*, I agreed readily. I needed the money; Sir William's estate was in ruins and, in moments of anxiety, I saw myself as a beggar in the street; only those with great ambitions know what great fears drive them forward. The opera was a burlesque merely, which satisfied a modern audience's taste for laughing at what it does not understand, but one of its characters, Bunthorne, was said to bear some resemblance to myself: that was of course why I had been asked to accompany the tour. But I was determined to rise to the occasion which offered itself to me, and assert the values of art and the imagination. If I was forced to travel as a missionary among cannibals, at least I would insist on devouring them.

When I saw New York from the deck of the steam-ship, I was repelled. It resembled a vast Swan and Edgar's, which seemed to be engaged in a perpetual sale. I came down upon the shore and was at once surrounded by a crowd of journalists. 'Here he is!' they shouted. 'Buffalo Bill!' I felt quite faint with anticipation, although I discovered that in New York anticipation can be indefinitely prolonged. I learned, on closer inspection, that it suffers from what Lombroso would call a disease of the spirit – an absence of imagination contracted from too close a proximity to horse-hair sofas and cast-iron stoves. But, if New York showed America at its most primitive, I found its real civilisation in the wilderness: the mining towns of the West and the small communities couched in the great plains of the interior mark quite a new phase in the development of contemporary life. Free of hypocrisy and the affectation of European values, they will become the engines of the modern period. I have always admired artlessness in others, and the Americans are fashioning a philosophy out of it which will rival Locke for its method and Rousseau for its self-confidence.

I travelled from lecture hall to lecture hall, and discovered in the process the secret of being a public performer: I talked to myself and the audience overheard me. I spoke of the House Beautiful and American domestic life was altered overnight; I described the Aesthetic Movement in Dress and the next day Attic creatures were seen in the streets. The women worshipped me and the men talked about me. I was compared to George Eliot, although in what respect I am not sure. The Americans are without traditions of any kind, and they treat with proper deference anyone who tells them where to go and what to do. The men would dig into a charnel pit if someone had informed them that gold was buried there, and the women would applaud them for their courage. But I offered them Ruskin and blue-and-white china instead; they accepted them with gratitude, and repaid me with strange green notes. I became a commercial proposition. My success came as a revelation to me: I discovered that I could earn considerable sums of money simply by being myself. But I became aware also of a peculiar but now to me familiar phenomenon: as soon as I had expressed my philosophy, I ceased to adhere to it. Once I had given perfect form to my ideas and attitudes, they became wearisome to me. When people believed in me, I ceased to believe in myself.

I can recall quite clearly the journey from Omaha to San Francisco which I made with the opera troupe; God had created the world in less time than it took us to travel across America. We travelled in a train so slow that young men in the third class carriages fired their revolvers at the small creatures who dwell on the prairies. I do not know if they were people or animals: perhaps they themselves were not entirely sure. During the journey I read French novels – the great advantage of really contemporary fiction is that one finds oneself mirrored on every page – but I slept in the heat of the afternoon: it is strange, is it not, how once I enjoyed sleep?

I woke one afternoon and left my compartment to purchase a sandwich, a fanciful lead-coloured thing, only to find John Howson, who played Bunthorne, that absurd caricature of myself, standing upon the observation platform dressed in a costume similar to my own and reciting one of my poems. We had stopped at a little station and the credulous population assumed at once that Howson was Wilde. I felt quite revolted.

'Howson!' I said when he had returned to our carriage. 'Do you remember me? I am Oscar Wilde. Do you recall, also, that we are travelling together? Or did you imagine that I had fallen off somewhere, and you were required to remedy the deficiency?'

'I'm sorry, Oscar, I couldn't resist it. When a chap is asleep, and another chap wants to have a bit of fun, it's forgivable, ain't it?'

'Howson, my dear boy. You are an actor. I understand actors. I do not have the slightest objection to your forgetting who you are, but it is not wise to adopt the personality of someone who is *sitting on the same train.*' I emphasised the last words by hitting his knee with *Mademoiselle de Maupin.*

'Oh really, Oscar, you are no better than me. At least I know when I am acting.'

'I am not an actor. I am myself.'

'Oh, yes, tell all.'

'That is all you need to know.'

'You came here as part of the troupe, Oscar, and hard luck if I steal the best scenes.'

'At least my lines are my own.'

'Excuse me, but they are not. I see you copying them from those books of yours, and rehearsing them when you sit on the you-know-what.'

'I don't have the faintest idea what you are talking about. At least I never strut around in borrowed finery and pretend that I am someone other than myself.'

'Nonsense. You have never been yourself.'

At this critical juncture, an official of the railway entered the carriage. 'Which of you is Mr Oscar Wilde?' he said.

'He is,' we both replied at once.

'I have a note from a lady to give to Mr Wilde.'

'Oh, let him have it,' I replied. I dislike 'notes', they are always so loud.

'I say, Wilde, here is a lady who wants to meet us – I mean, meet you – when we reach San Francisco. Shall I reply?'

'Tell her that I am otherwise engaged.'

'Oh, be a sport, Oscar. Why not let me go in your place?'

'You have gone so far already, Howson, that I can hardly stop you.'

And so it was that the American newspapers were full of my activities as a ladies' man: it was Howson. And, when he was discovered by journalists in a New York gambling den, he again used my name. As a result, reports that I frequented such places even reached England. I never cared to contradict them: who was I to stand in the path of my destiny? I felt like Adah Menken, doomed to lead the life which others imagined for me. But just as my philosophy had ceased to interest me as soon as it was formulated into a set of principles so, when I saw myself being imitated, I realised at once what an incubus my aesthetic personality might become if I were to be trapped within it. Imitation changes, not the impersonator, but the impersonated.

And, indeed, in that country where all the modern miracles will occur, my personality did develop. In America I acquired a certain ease and freedom of manner which were denied to me in England. For the first time my work was taken seriously: where before I had been an object of scorn or gossip, known principally as a companion of the famous, now I was hailed as an artist. I was interviewed continually, and my poetry was published in the better newspapers at a guinea a line. When I had made that discovery, when I realised that it was in my art that others might recognise me, I felt quite free. The sensation, when it is at last woken in a young man, resembles that of being propelled by a vast gale – forward, but without any ostensible goal; like a ship as it leaves harbour, slowly the cries and the greetings from the shore die away, and one is at last silently travelling amid the immensity of the sea and the sky. It is then, and only then, that one can impart form to the imagination and life to the fluttering wings of the spirit.

When I met Whitman, therefore, I came to him not as a disciple but as an equal – the only situation in which true artists can ever meet. I visited the wide, bright attic in Philadelphia where he sat like an American patriarch; behind him I could see the tall white sails of ships upon the Delaware but they were pleasantly obscured by the smoke which issued from the factory chimneys.

Our conversation was affable and easy. Whitman had never travelled to Europe, so he had retained his perfect manners – but he had shrewdness, also, the shrewdness which saw the writer even then coming to birth within me. I told him that I had come to lecture to his countrymen on the Beautiful.

'It seems to me, Oscar,' he said, 'that the beautiful is not an abstraction to make a gallop for, but really an effect of what you produce.'

'But surely the Beautiful is also an ideal?'

He had a curious giggle in his voice, as though he had swallowed a genie which was quite content to stay where it was. 'Ideals are hobgoblins,' he replied. 'If you search for them, they lead you astray and into the swamp. If you let them come to you, they will be true companions.'

I realise only now the truth of what he said to me then: the search for Beauty has had terrible consequences for me. In my days of fame I hunted for it in every guise and, in my eagerness to grasp it, I quite mistook its nature. And so Beauty turned from me and left me in the shadows, in the second circle of Hell where I may meet Dido and Semiramis face to face.

That is all I have to say about America: now it is time for luncheon.

30 August 1900

Society frightens me, but solitude disturbs me more. I feel it all the more acutely in a hotel such as this. I live in disorder for 90 francs a month, in a room which is saved from the horror of a boudoir only by a very high ceiling. The furnishings have faded to a disagreeable shade of burgundy, and the wallpaper is one of the few remaining victims of the *ancien régime*. How I long for Lincrusta Walton. I had my smoking room in Tite Street covered with that material, and I always believed that I gained inspiration from its peculiar mottled surface. I would run my hand against it and, much to the indignation of my wife, tear off little strips and place them in my mouth as I wrote. I suppose that I have always eaten that which is dear to me.

There is a mirror in my room here, but I never look into it: the mirror itself would be quite safe, of course, but I might crack. Next to it there rests an ormolu clock decorated with sham onyxes: it is far too large, and too ornate for its purpose. It bears all the marks of time while remaining implacably solemn: even if it knew that it was going to be destroyed on the next hour, it would keep on striking until that hour came. And my friends wonder why I have grown so fond of it!

I possess also an iron bed with four copper balls mounted upon it, a small bookcase carved out of a wood so dark that it quite matches the books, a combination of washstand and chest-of-drawers, a table covered with red cloth on which I am writing at the moment, one wooden chair where I now sit, and two 'Armenian armchairs' which can be purchased for twelve francs at the Bazaar de l'Hôtel de Ville. A linoleum carpet completes the picture: it is hard on one's shoes, and also rather a strain on one's imagination.

Have I told you that I am now in constant pain from my ear? There is nothing to do with one's burdens except pass them on and so I sent a message to Maurice inviting him to lunch – he only listens to my bad news after he has been fed – but I have as yet received no answer. I have become accustomed to his presence on certain occasions each week and now, with my imagination in disorder and my life in ruins, it is not strange that I should cling to the trivial order of daily events. I shave each morning, for example, and I dress with care, arranging my limited wardrobe of Doré suits with effects that even Ada Rehan might wonder at. Then I light a cigarette and, if I have nothing wonderful to say, I write this journal.

My food is always the same. At nine o'clock I have coffee and a roll with butter. At luncheon, two hard-boiled eggs and a chop of mutton. In the summer, I pass my afternoon reading in the courtyard of the hotel. There are two trees there which shade me, and we speak of many things. The wind, however, has recently grown jealous of our intimacy and blows upon my ear in a quite painful manner.

Earlier in the year, I passed my days at the Exhibition, like Iphigeneia among the barbarians: although, alas, I am my own sacrifice. Half the strength of the modern period comes from its entire lack of a sense of humour, and so I was sadly out of place there. The tourists would sneer at me, and there would be whisperings behind my back. In order to disguise myself I bought a camera, but I was at once deprived of all powers of sight and started taking pictures of the Louvre.

I understand now why certain Eastern deities are too holy to be represented by an image – there is an element of perverse ingenuity in the photograph which robs one's friends of reality and reduces architecture to a shadow. Of course I have no objection myself to being photographed: I owe so little to realism now that I am the perfect subject and, fortunately, I rarely move. Alas, in a moment of generosity, I gave my camera to a boy in Rome who begged for it as though it were a papal blessing – no doubt it will become one. In any case, in Paris I haunt places where a camera would be quite unsuitable.

Only yesterday evening, for example, Maurice led me to the Château Rouge. I told him that I had been to that café many times in my youth, and he looked at me with astonishment. The young never understand youth in others: that is their tragedy. The old do, always: that is theirs. But I had never before entered the large room above the public area. I had heard of it, naturally: it is where the poor and the vagabond sleep, and for the first time I was moved by curiosity to see it. Perhaps it is where one day I will rest my own head.

I mounted a flight of wooden steps and entered the attic. Here huddled before me were the outcasts of the city. The place is called popularly 'The Morgue' or 'La Salle des Morts', and no more appropriate name could have been given to it. It lends to it that element of dignity – the dignity of last, extreme things – which wretchedness seems to me always to possess: Jesus became an outcast in order that he might represent the true image of mankind. And, where once I would have shrunk back in horror from the sight, now I looked on with interest. I have seen into the heart of the world: why should I not look upon its face also?

That is why I wander. I am not a Bohemian by temperament – only, you might say, by conviction. My friends tell me that I am disordered and wasteful of my talent but I have been explaining, have I not, that I lead a quite ordinary life? I leave the courtyard when the trees whisper to me of evening, and go to my room to change. I dine in restaurants for two or three francs on éperlans frits. When I am in funds I go to Sylvain's for truite à la rivière, the rouget and the choux à la crème, and then I proceed to the Grand Café where I watch the primitive tragedies of real life. I meet artists and writers in Pousset's. I go to Maire's for the brandy, the Café de la Paix for conversation and the Kalisaya for love. Here we shock the tourists by speaking 'with a difference'. In the Kalisaya are whispered the secrets of Paris – so secret, indeed, that they are often quite untrue.

Sometimes, after a more than usually agreeable evening, I am smuggled to the Quartier Latin where by some strange paradox we speak of Greek things. The company is not always immaculate: some of them believe literature to consist entirely of stories from the *Petit Journal*. I do not disabuse them of this charming notion, since they would lose all sense of their own importance if I did so. I do not return until late and I make a point of never carrying money home with me: it would only be wasted. As Baudelaire put it in a moment of unusual clarity, 'Le superflu était le nécessaire.' Sometimes I return with vine-leaves in my hair; sometimes, even, with an entire harvest.

I give myself, I admit it, to the companionship of drink and boys; the boys are more expensive but, then, they are far more mature. In truth·drink has the better effect, for I am told that it prevents me from becoming boring. Some people drink to forget, I drink to remember. I drink in order to understand what I mean and to discover what I know. Under its benign influence all the stories and dramas which properly belong to the sphere of art are announced by me in conversation. I am walking evidence that oral literature did not perish with Homer, for I carry my verses in my mouth and in my heart. Sometimes, towards the end of the evening, I see a light coming towards me like the light that moved towards Dante and led him towards Purgatory. But I imagine I am in Paradise – I believe that, in these moods, my companions find me rather wonderful.

Drink has always held a terrible fascination for me. It is some strange fatality carried in the blood: my mother, in her loneliness, grew to depend on brown and opal liquids with curious names, and I am told that Willie died from the effects of excessive whisky. It was absinthe which I drank last night with Maurice: absinthe removes the bitter taste of failure and grants me strange visions which are charming principally because they cannot be written down. Only in absinthe do I become entirely free and, when I drink it, I understand the symbolic mysteries of odour and of colour. It is strangely reminiscent of the essence santonin which, even in small quantities, allows one to see violet in all things. Small quantities of Maeterlinck have, I am told, a similar effect.

But at these times I feel the burden of my existence lifted from me: everything has happened as it should happen. Whatever is realised is right. I think I shall write an essay, 'In Defence of Drunkenness', to be handed to the faithful – but only after they have completed their devotions. Where is Maurice?

31 August 1900

I have a copy of *Les Misérables* here in my room. Since, like the urchin, I have been thrown upon the streets, it has become my Baedeker for the really interesting aspects of French society. The book is now quite as battered as its owner; I bought it when I first came to Paris, and it has a signature as large and as florid as some monstrous orchid: Oscar Wilde, March 1883.

I had returned from America, determined that I was to begin a new life, the life of an artist. But when I arrived in London I found only the old personality which I had thought to transcend. It would have been impossible for me to do serious work in an atmosphere which I had left charged with the temperament of the *blagueur*. I went to live with my mother, but the shades of infancy hovered over my head and would have crushed the laurels which I wished to place there. When I was with her, it was as if any achievement of mine would count for nothing.

And so I fled my mother's house, and travelled to Paris. This city seemed to me then to be the centre of European literary civilisation. Of course I had read the French poets of the modern school – Coppée, Rechepin and Mallarmé were interesting in the days before they were understood – but it was the masters of French prose to whom I owed the greatest debt. When I was an undergraduate I had discovered Victor Hugo: here was a writer who knew pity and understood, also, the awful solitude of suffering, the solitude of the human soul which does not know itself. I was too young to learn from the mystery of that suffering, but I understood perfectly the miraculous prose of the poet.

I had read Baudelaire and was entranced by his prose, just as later I was to be captivated by the poetry of *A Rebours*, with its strange scents and colours. Huysmans is, in the modern period, the great prophet of artifice – of that coming age in which nature will have exhausted all of her powers, and the artist paints her most vivid effects for her. In the dimly lit pages of that book I first saw Salomé rise up, covered in opals and in hydrophanes.

I loved Gautier's work also. He once wrote a play in which Elogabolus throws himself into a water closet: an effect I have always wanted to use upon the stage. His novel, *Mademoiselle de Maupin*, awoke wonderful dreams in me for I, too, had experienced the sensations of its hero when, trembling upon the abyss of a fiery-coloured passion, he is no longer certain who he is or who others are. I wished, in those days, to write a novel of the heart in Gautier's manner, a book of strange sins whose father would be Werther and whose mother Manon Lescaut. And indeed I have always attempted to express in my own tongue the languor and the eroticism of French writers. Their sentences are like flowers pressed tightly together: no light can pass through them which is not dazed by colour and infected by scent. And there were others: I worshipped Flaubert with my head, Stendhal with my heart, and Balzac by my manner of dress. When I moved into the Hôtel Voltaire I adopted a white dressing gown, in which I would sit up through the night to continue my writing.

Of course Balzac sees life as it is, fashioning it into shape as a sculptor will fashion stone into a beautiful form. I saw life then as a parade of shadows intoning strange syllables. The fact is that I did not know life at all.

I remember a story. There was once a poet who sang of the secret things of the world. The music of his verses was forever chanted in the city, and those whom he met stepped back to let him pass. Each morning, at dawn, he would rise up from his solitary bed – for poets, in their imagination at least, always sleep alone – and walk into the desert beyond the city. It was a trackless waste but the poet recognised his way and he walked on until he came to one rock and a tree which shaded it. Here he would sit and, stooping down towards the sand, he would let the grains sift through his fingers. Then he would lift up his head and gaze at the tawny horizon of the desert, at the great wilderness which has no shade and no movement. When he grew tired of staring, he would raise his eyes to the sky which shone like beaten copper over the desert. No birds flew here, and no cloud distracted his gaze.

So he would pass the day and, when the shadow of the tree told him that evening approached, he would rise from his rock and return to the city. As always, at the end of the day, when the people saw him walking with firm step towards the great gate of the city, they would come out to greet him and, after words of salutation, they would question him eagerly. 'Tell us, what have you seen today? What visions of terror and of beauty?' And then he would reply, and tell them what he had seen. 'I have seen the scarlet Ibis carry a star in her beak, and I have seen the giant Lizard expire and turn into bronze. A young Nereid rose from the sand; when I embraced her, she turned into a wave of the sea. All these, and other things, have I seen.' And they marvelled at what the poet had told them; the common people wondered where they might find the giant Lizard of bronze, while the priests of the city saw in the poet's words a shadowy image of spiritual things. But the poet was greatly feared, and no one questioned him about the interpretation of such matters.

Another dawn came, and the poet walked across the desert to his usual rock, and under the shade of the same tree he bent down and gazed upon the sand. But as he did so remorse stepped over his heart as if it were a lizard of bronze. 'I have destroyed all those who loved me,' he said, 'I rose from their beds at dawn and never turned my head. I have heard them weeping, and I have walked away into this desert place.' And then the poet turned his eyes towards the horizon, and saw the shadows of his own life. 'I have lied to all those who listen to me. I have given them tawdry images for the sake of gold. In order to find praise, I have invented the secrets of the world.' And then he turned his face towards the blank sky, and saw only the emptiness of his own life. 'I see my life now as a vacant listening to the wind, a hollow straw which falls slowly to the ground.'

And the poet gathered up his cloak and returned to the city, for it was evening now. 'What have you seen today? What have you seen today?' they asked him, and he would not answer. But they kept up their clamouring until at last he spoke to them. 'I have seen nothing,' he told them, 'I have seen nothing today.' For the first time, the poet had seen reality and he could not speak of it. And then they jeered at him, and some of them picked up stones to hurl at his back as he returned slowly to his own dwelling.

When I told Robbie this story, he asked me to write it down. He promised an American newspaper. Of course he had not understood.

1 September 1900

I was in the Hôtel Voltaire, was I not, in a white dressing gown? My room looked out over the Seine and I learned at once one of the first principles of the creative imagination: an artist should never have a view. It is so deceptive. So I ignored the river and wrote my second play, *The Duchess of Padua*, a fantastic Jacobean thing. As I wrote it, I felt the spirits of the great dead quick within me but, unfortunately, most of them died a second time. It was not a success, and is notable now only for the number of costume changes I introduced. But in those days I was never more serious than when I was using melodrama. It has since become the basis of all my commercial correspondence but I realise now that it has no part in literature. And yet I understood through the failure of that play a more significant truth: as soon as I took my own work seriously I was laughed at and my words ridiculed. If I was to succeed as an artist, and find an audience for my art, I would have to proceed by cunning obliquity – by the guile of the creative artist who smiles where others weep and who sheds bitter tears while all those around him are lost in laughter.

I came to Paris as that remarkable creature, a disciple. I have always believed that it is only in association with others that one finds oneself – and, for an artist, contact with other artists is absolutely necessary for the growth of his personality. And so I set out to meet everyone; my volume of Poems was my introduction, and, indeed, I needed no other. If I seemed brash, it was only the brashness of high spirits: as soon as the soil of England was wiped from my feet, I walked with quicker and lighter step.

In the cafés, in those apricot-coloured days, one met all the young poets – or at least the poets who considered themselves young. The French writers seemed to be ahead of me, and I became involved in what I thought then to be a great movement in art and letters. I was closest to Barbey d'Aurevilly. He had a disagreeable room in the Rue Rousselet, close to where Maurice is now living. The first time I called upon him, he came to the door in a suspiciously silk dressing gown and then, waving his arm around a bare and dirty room, announced that 'I have sent my household effects into the country'. Only a true artist can banish reality with one magnificent gesture.

Often, at the Café Cénacle, I would see Verlaine, like a Silenus carved in butter. On the first occasion we met, he had been granted a day's exeat from the hospital where he was being treated, I believe, for the sins of Venus. He showed me an ulcer upon his leg, and giggled. I felt quite faint: physical ugliness has always been abhorrent to me and I tried afterwards to avoid him, but he always assumed a jovial intimacy and sat beside me, as though we were linked by bonds invisible to our companions.

I would sometimes meet him in Mallarmé's rooms in the Rue de Rome. I remember quite clearly the first time I visited Mallarmé – really, it was as if one was attending a séance. Whistler had heard that I was coming to Paris, and had tried to turn Mallarmé against me; he is too ridiculous. When it became clear, however, that Mallarmé, a poet, a lord of language, would of course welcome me, Whistler sent him a telegram. 'Wilde viendra chez vous. Serrez l'argenterie.' I once painted a likeness of Whistler in one of my stories. I told him so one evening, and he assumed at once I meant Lord Henry Wotton. In fact, I had the Remarkable Rocket in mind.

That first evening with Mallarmé was something of a success: my French is, I am told, somewhat florid and literary but I was understood perfectly by my peers: indeed I believe I would have been understood if I had said nothing at all. Mallarmé was immensely courteous, and affable, slow of speech as all poets should be, but with a most remarkable purity of diction. *Contes cruels* had just been published – now it is just being read – and I remember Mallarmé praising that wonderful volume to me as containing 'les tristesses, la solitude, les déboires'. His voice was like a bell tolling in the distance.

The quiet flow of conversation, the sombre ornate furniture, all spread a strange torpor over one's senses so that the only matters of any importance were Art and the things of Art. Flaubert was there, with the flushed cheeks and moustache of a Viking. It was entirely characteristic of him that he expressed an affection for Caliban. I have often been struck by the apparent insignificance of the greatest artists, for it seems to me that they lack self-awareness. Flaubert's writing is quite cold but with a coldness that in its ferocity burns – like the embrace of the devil which, in books of medieval magic, is so intensely cold that it is described as fiery. But to hear him talk – well, one might have been listening to the conversation of a pork butcher. That is nothing against his art: indeed, in my own case, if my love for art had been more intense than my love of fame and of sensation, I might have created much greater things. I feel like Andrea del Sarto in Browning's exquisite poem,

> Had I been two, another and myself,
> Our work would have o'erlooked the world.

As it is, my personality has destroyed my work: that is the one unforgivable sin of my life. Even in those first months in Paris, my affection for luxury and for fame beguiled me from the company of those artists at whose feet I should have sat. Instead, I lived in fiacres and restaurants; I was fêted in the salons of the Baronne Deslandes and the Princess de Monaco, that strange Siren without a voice and, indeed, hardly a country. I accompanied Sarah Bernhardt from her dressing room to the edge of the stage – and always the heady, sweet smell of triumph, the spectacle of purple and of gold, led me fatally forward. With poets and artists I felt that only part of my temperament was truly engaged: in some ways I stood apart from them for I felt even then that my destiny was to be greater than theirs. With Sarah I felt that I, like her, could triumph over the world: the brilliant receptions, the dinners, the life of a great personality, these were the things I most desired.

I shared my enthusiasm in those early days with Robert Sherard, a young Englishman whom I had met at dinner. He had the looks of a fallen angel: now, of course, he has quite completed the process and insists that his friends descend with him. But then he was full of impossible dreams and, since he had impossible youthfulness also, I had great affection for him.

I once explained to him that my three favourite characters in fiction were Julien Sorel, Lucien de Rubempré and myself. Like de Rubempré, I told him, I wanted 'd'être celébré et d'être aimé', and like Sorel, I would sometimes cry out in anguish, 'Pourquoi suis-je moi?' I can recall quite clearly walking along the Seine with Robert one evening and recounting in inordinate detail the last hours of Sorel in a prison cell; how lost he was in a mist of words and how, in the last extreme moments before his death, all he heard within himself were broken sentences from the books he had loved, the books upon which he had modelled his character. Lucien hanged himself, and Julien died on the scaffold. 'But then, Robert,' I warned him, 'these were the lives of the saints.'

I was fascinated in those days also by Chatterton, Poe, Baudelaire and by the horror of their fate – when you are young, you play with the fire which you do not understand. The death of Chatterton still brings tears to my eyes – with scarcely bread to feed himself but charged with the knowledge of fame to come, a strange, slight boy who was so prodigal of his genius that he attached the names of others to it. It is the great tragedy of the eighteenth century, with the possible exception of Pope's verses.

But, if in Chatterton I heard the sad music of human hopefulness, in the fate of Poe I heard the strange laughter of the gods who give men the instruments of torture with which they tear themselves to pieces. I peered into the abyss and looked down upon those whose personalities had been destroyed or quite twisted out of shape, and I felt a strange elation. With Sherard I visited the Rue de la Vieille Lanterne where de Nerval hanged himself: for me, each cobble seemed enchanted. It was as if we had come to an archaic place where blood had been spilt in sacrifice. Sherard did not understand such things – he was too romantic to have a proper sense of fate. Once, I remember, we went to the rooms of Maurice Rollinat; Rollinat began reciting to us his soliloquy of Troppman, a grotesque, dark piece of writing. He screamed and cursed, beating the ground with his feet. Sherard looked at me appalled. But I thought it wonderful – it was the mad dance of the artist in his own wound, a scream of rage and defiance in which I wished to add my own voice.

I am surprised that no one has yet written a shilling treatise on the effect of poetry upon conduct – although I suppose that Matthew Arnold is presumed to have the last word on such subjects. Of course, when one reads him, one always hopes that every word will be his last. I could write such a treatise with some conviction, for it seems to me that only when I read French poetry did I begin to seek eagerly for those sensations that might provoke in me that despair which I cherished in the writings of others. In Huysmans' book, Des Esseintes keeps three of Baudelaire's poems under glass – 'La Mort des Amants', 'Anywhere Out of the

World' and 'L'Ennemi'. In those three is contained the entire history of modern feeling and it was under the spell of Baudelaire's sonorous anguish that I set out, for the first time, to explore the dark quarters of the world.

With Sherard, and the young French poets, I would haunt the most disreputable taverns and associate with the common people of the streets. In London and in America that world had been unknown to me, and the first experience of it in Paris awakened in me the taste for more and wilder delights. I was like Pasiphae who had seen the monster and cries to see it again. In my imagination this city was both Babylon and Parnassus; it was a sea from which some god might rise to claim me but, for a time, I was content to drown in its waters.

And so we would travel to distant places where Sapphists lurked, where girls or boys could be bought and enjoyed. Of course I did nothing then; I was, I think, too frightened. Indeed so strongly did I feel within myself the terrible fascination of such things that in the end I fled from those strange passions stalking in the chambers of my heart. I determined to leave Paris. I had seen too many of those who, having tasted the Lotus, fall into lethargy and despair. With the self-confidence of youth I was determined to preserve myself but I knew also that, having acquired the knowledge of forbidden things, I could go back to England and become great.

3 September 1900

Robert Sherard approached me in the Pied Noir last night and, in a state of some intoxication, announced that he wished to write my biography.

'I will weave a crown for your head, Oscar,' he told me.

'What is the use of a crown without royalties, Bobbie?'

I was a little short with him but he becomes less interesting nightly. He would write a biography, he said, which would explain my conduct to the world and reveal my true character.

'You will defend me at the cost of my reputation,' I told him. But, as always, he paid no attention.

'Do you remember our early days in Paris, when we read Poe and Chatterton together?'

'I recall nothing whatever, Robert. There is one principle you must understand if you insist upon this absurd undertaking: an artist's life is determined by what he forgets, not by what he remembers.'

'Why must you laugh at everything, Oscar?'

'Well, Robert, I am told that Plato died with the farces of Sophron under his pillow. Only I have your company instead.'

He staggered off in the general direction of absinthe; I hope never to see him again.

After such encounters, I feel acutely the waste of everything I might have become. Sometimes I feel compelled to gaze upon my fate like Regulus, with his lids cut off, who was forced to look upon the sun until his eyes withered and died. And I, who once kissed the goddess of fortune, now lie down in the stews with only the ghosts of my past for companions. Every success has been fateful to me, so that my life has rocked continually on the knees of the gods. In my brilliant days, my fortune was so great that it filled me with fear. But, since I ran willingly towards my destiny, I forgot sometimes that I was the victim. I was the ox fattened with flowers, but for the sacrifice only.

I wrote once in *Dorian Gray*, 'to say a thing is to bring it to pass', and then I crossed the phrase out. The world does not know of it because I did not want the world to understand one of the secrets of my art. It is a strange thing, but in all my writing I anticipate my own fate. Everything that has happened to me – even the beautiful spring day when I was released from the winter of prison – is mentioned somewhere in my work. I saw Nemesis and I placed its nets around my shoulders. I think I have explained how, in my earliest years, I was taken to see the Galway woman who read my hand. And, although I forgot her prophecies in the midst of boyish pleasures, I understood even then that my secret history was already written and that nothing I might do or say could alter it in the slightest particular.

And so throughout my life I have consulted volumes of magic, chiromancy and cabbalistic lore, to see if I might pierce the heart of the mystery which surrounds me. I read Andreae's *The Chemical Wedding*, that poisoned flower of German baroque literature, the *Secrets* of Weckerus and the *Artis Cabalisticae* of John Pistorius. In that febrile air where fate reveals its mysteries, I was comforted only by Paracelsus's device: 'Be not another, if thou canst be thyself.'

I have always also consulted the secretaries to the gods – the palmists, or psalmists as Bosie calls them, are now so important to our civilisation that one always met them at dinner parties, although on those occasions one knew one's fate in advance. I once met Cheiro at one of his informal 'evenings' at Lady Colin Campbell's. I put my hand through a curtain so that he could not see my face. As always I trembled with apprehension: at these moments, I feel that my past life means nothing and that I am to be reborn. 'The left hand,' Cheiro told me, 'is the hand of a king. The right hand is that of a king who will send himself into exile.' I was asked by others what he had said to me, but I could not speak. At the end of the evening, when he emerged from behind his curtain like a character in some Adelphi melodrama, I could not look at him or approach him. But he seemed to catch my eye: I stared at him, and he gave me a most curious glance. It was after that occasion that I wrote *Lord Arthur Savile's Crime*, in which the palmist sees the improbable shape of his own death in the hand of another. It was, I suppose, my way of laughing at Fate.

And yet I cannot escape it. At moments of crisis in my life, I have always consulted those who know. I used to see Mrs

Robinson regularly in London, and I wrote to her just before my trial. She prophesied success – the gods are cruel. Only last year I tempted them again to wilder laughter. I went, with More Adey, to a famous fortune teller here. She looked at my hand, and then said in the most polite manner, 'I am puzzled. By your line of life, you died two years ago.'

I still have my scarab ring. I had just returned from Paris and I was wandering down Holywell Lane, a narrow street full of shops which sold curiosities and the battered relics of dispersed libraries. I was in one of these shops, glancing at some more than usually revolting glassware, when a young man entered, rather breathlessly, and asked to see its owner. He was a working man; he was employed at Billingsgate, gutting fish, he said. I remember the phrase caught my attention. He had found this, he said, on the floor of the market, and was it worth anything – and then he held out the ring which now I wear. The owner inspected it and, being a man of no particular discernment, offered him a shilling. The young man took offence at this, and left the shop.

I followed him outside and asked to see the ring myself, and he proffered it to me. I could see at once the wonder of its green stone – I offered him five pounds, which of course he accepted. 'Where did you find this, exactly?' I asked him. 'I told the governor, on the floor.' And then he laughed: 'Perhaps a fish brought it.' Since that time, the scarab has been precious to me. I showed it to John Farrell, the expert in Egyptology at the British Museum, and he assured me that it was the ring of a high official in that empire. I did not tell him where I had found it: it would have sounded somewhat too mythological. But its strange origins haunted me and I felt that it might, like Edgar Poe's gold bug, lead me to great fortune – a fortune dancing attendance upon violence and mortality. Indeed it drew me even closer to Poe's sweet sense of fate for, when I returned to London from Paris, I saw the life of the sewers with awakened eyes. I felt myself like him drawn towards the precipice, imagining the sensations of my fall: and so, in the end, I plunged down and was destroyed.

4 September 1900

The pain in my head woke me this morning and, as I raised myself from the bed in agony, I saw on my pillow noxious substances discharged from my ear. I am used to this now but, when I first saw the blood and the mucus, I felt the horror of one whose life is visibly ebbing away; but now I am in so continuously weak and painful a state that I do not lament the stages in my decline. I merely watch them with interest.

I injured my ear in Wandsworth prison. I had been kept in my cell because of my general sickness and anguish until the prison doctor, examining me, told me that I must take some exercise in the yard. 'It will do you good,' he said. 'It will stop you thinking about yourself.' Such is the banality of those who work in places of evil. And so I was escorted down the metal steps, across the metal landing, and the door of the courtyard was opened for me. I saw the light, and I watched the prisoners walking around the yard. In my cell I could hide and weep; but I felt the daylight like a sword, and I fell. My ear was damaged in that fall: it has become my relic from prison, a stigma which bleeds, not once a year at festivals, but every night. I must stop now: I am in such pain that I must send again for the little Jewish doctor.

He has come. He has a wonderful gift for changing his mind and, where once he diagnosed neurasthenia, now he suspects something worse. He has told me that I must prepare myself for an operation, and has left a phial of chloral to comfort me. Later he promises me morphia, when I cry to dream again. I am used to narcotics. Sometimes, when I lie in their embrace, I see my personality rising out of me and going to hide in some corner of the room until it is sure it is quite safe to return. In these moods I resemble Mr Wells's Invisible Man – only recognisable to myself, and to others, when I am dressed.

72

Recently, however, these nerve sedatives have alarmed me with their power. I remember once, some years ago in London, being taken by an angel of the streets to Brick Lane, to one of those houses of shame where opium is bought and sold. I was led to an upstairs room – it was large and unhealthy, a lime pit where the diseased are buried – and I saw there only grinning phantoms, men who neither woke nor slept; they lived somewhere out of the world, and the looks they cast were terrible: I had been thrown among blind men who had put out each other's eyes. I turned away in horror – some sights of the world resemble those when we glimpse the Gorgon, but alas the world does not turn us to stone – but now I find myself being drawn ineluctably towards the same fate. Perhaps it is not a fearful one: perhaps the gods are wise to take away our wits before they destroy us.

After I have taken chloral, I no longer sleep even in the pit of the night. I lie in a daze and watch absurd shapes pass in phantasmagoric array. I know that, when I return to my bed after writing this, little lizards will chase each other through my brain. But I also run: I am both hunter and hunted, watcher and watched. I will take the chloral now.

I am afraid to grasp sleep even when it is offered to me: I have such bad dreams, dreams which do not leave my waking moments. Once I dreamt that I seemed to be a mask lying on the counter of a shop in Piccadilly. Many people came in and tried me upon their faces: I saw myself reflected in the mirrors, a strange white thing, but then they laughed and flung me back upon the counter. I jerked awake, and I was panting for breath.

Is it possible that in my dreams I have become the artist that I have ceased to be in my ordinary hours? Is it possible that, now I have been torn apart, mine is the song of Marsyas rather than Apollo and that through pain I acquire prophecy? I dreamed of two lambs, and then of a fawn with one of its legs cut off, its life blood dripping upon the grass. The next morning, I received in the post a photograph of my two children – I wept when I saw in them the lineaments of my own face, as it might have been when I was a child – and in a daze of sorrow I walked out into the streets. A young man limped along on the other side of the Rue des Beaux Arts: his leg had been sawn off at the hip. Is it the secret of dreams that they prefigure reality and thus help us to endure it, that they turn a child into a lamb and a suffering spirit into a fawn? It would explain, at least, the somewhat obscure origins of mythology, all those sad stories which mimic human reality and bear it aloft like a bier.

The night before she died, my wife Constance herself appeared before me in a dream, walking towards me with her hands outstretched, and I called out, 'Go away! Go away!'; whether in pity or in anger I do not know.

It seems to me that the pain I experience on waking is the pain of knowing one's mortality; in sleep I return to the enchanted, terrible world of childhood in which joys are more joyful, horrors more horrible, because there is no consciousness that they will end.

In these fiery-coloured visions, my mother is the dominant note. She flashes across them darkly: other faces, even that of Constance, become her face; other hands become her hands. And how could it not be so? I resemble her in so many things. Sometimes I think that all the best in me was woven from her. It was she who gave birth to that mysterious essence which dwells in me and from which my thoughts were born, and from those thoughts my art once sprang. In my old days, I would find myself imitating her gestures and her manners and, when I wrote, it seems to me now that hers was the image which, like a ghost in the forest, I always glimpsed within my words. The chloral is working within me now. I must rest for a moment: I always enjoy familiar sensations.

Salomé was, for me, the ideal woman: lust is terrible and, in her madness, she destroys the man who denies that lust. My male characters belong to the sphere of fancy merely – my women belong to the sphere of art. I have always preferred my heroines – I understand them because I was terrified of them. Only they can afford to be serious, because they see life as a game. If I had been a woman, there is no knowing to what heights I might have reached. The chloral is cold, with the coldness of the polar regions which makes one drowsy. I will sleep now. I see monstrous butterflies coming to rest on my face. I see the shapes of monsters everywhere – beautiful monsters, too large, too large for ourselves.

5 September 1900

I must not lose the thread of this narrative: I must master the past by giving it the meaning which only now it possesses for me. I had left Paris, had I not, and come back to London? I was penniless, but I was the prodigal son who is allowed to return home as long as he remains prodigal; and so, in order to retain the position which I had assumed, I was compelled to set to work. I pawned my Gold Medal from Trinity and lectured upon America in the North of England: I do not know which caused me the greater pain.

I first met my wife, Constance, in Dublin, in the autumn of that year. Poor Constance, the last time I saw her was in prison. We discussed Cyril and Vyvyan but we did not talk about each other for there was, really, nothing left to say. I had said, and lied, too much to her in the past. She looked at me with pity in that dreadful place but it was I who pitied her – I had descended into Hell through my own vanity and weakness but she, unknowing, had been taken there.

I visited her grave in Genoa last year. It lies in a small cemetery outside the town, surrounded by wonderful wild flowers, and I was so moved by the sight that I asked the cabman to wait. I was seized with a fit of weeping but a sense, also, of the uselessness of weeping. Life is simple: the simple things happen always. I killed her just as surely as if I had fed her poison from a spoon. And now my name is not even on the stone which marks her grave.

My friends often asked me why I married her, and I used to reply that it was merely to find out what she thought of me; but, in truth, I knew that well enough. She loved me, that is all, and it is difficult to resist a love which is as innocent as it is unselfish. I saw myself as a romantic figure – not like Werther, who finds power in love, but like Pelleas, who finds salvation. I married Constance because I was afraid – afraid of what I might have become alone, of the desires which, if I had yielded to them, I would not have been able to control. I wished to build my life, not destroy it as I had seen others destroyed in Paris, and marriage to Constance was one means of doing so. If she was an angel, as I informed my friends, she was one who with flaming sword kept me from a paradise of forbidden pleasures.

My mother approved of the match. Constance was beautiful – women are always susceptible to the beauty of others. She was pale and very slim – my mother said she had the figure of a boy, but I pretended not to understand her. And she came from a fine Irish family. Really, I might have been performing a service to the nation. But I have always listened to my mother's advice – she possessed a shrewd common sense, at least in matters which did not concern herself, which, combined with her decidedly theatrical manner, was quite merciless. They became close friends: they would shop together and on the evenings when I was not at home, evenings which became too frequent, they would sit and talk about the children, or about Madame Blavatsky. My mother supported Constance until the end, until the burden of grief became too great even for her to hold.

Constance revered the idea of marriage: she had a vision of the heart guarded, if not by Penates, at least by a bamboo tea-table and a floriated carpet. She tried to influence me in that direction but I have always loathed modern domesticity, the life of the villas where they play waltz music and shop for their feelings in the circulating libraries. And so, in the little house we bought in Tite Street, we moved quite away from conventional interiors: it seems hard to recall but in those days, in the early Eighties, you could not have mahogany tables without magazines, or magazines without mahogany tables. With the help of Godwin we created in Chelsea a set of beautiful interiors: they took six months to fashion, one sordid and bitter afternoon to be destroyed by my creditors.

Tite Street is hideous, of course. All streets in London are. My friends told me that by living there I had become suburban, but I told them I was like the railway company – London *and* suburban. I can still see each room in that house: my study, with its statue of Hermes Praxiteles and the desk on which Carlyle wrote that wonderful, imaginary autobiography, *Sartor Resartus*, the dining room with Whistler's extraordinary ceiling, the drawing room where Constance and I would sit, in the early days of our marriage, in silent companionship. We had a piano there, and

76

sometimes Constance would play for me the popular songs; it amused her to hear me sing them, for even then I could invest the most banal sentiment with a wealth of feeling.

Some of my acquaintances abandoned me after my marriage: Frank Miles was absurd enough to think I had betrayed him. Others did not understand Constance: because she was quiet, they thought her dull. She was indeed silent in their company, but she was never dull about them afterwards. Some of the most trenchant comments about my friends came, not from the judges in the Old Bailey, but from her. She was not witty, but she was amusing. She was not an advanced woman – her lessons came from Wilde, not from Ibsen. I guided her in everything: she had a poetical nature, but she was still searching for the poetry with which to fill it. I placed beautifully bound books in her hands; we would visit the Grosvenor Gallery, not to look but to be looked at, for I have always considered myself to be an example of modern art; we would travel to Regent Street and I would choose the material for the dresses which I designed for her. It saddens me now, however, to think of the extraordinary compliance of her nature – I stiffened it, and then I broke it.

But in the early years of our marriage Constance was at peace: she used to sing to herself, and often seemed so perfectly happy that I was afraid to come near her. But she had a nervous habit of stroking her hair with her left hand, and would sometimes retreat into silences which were so sudden that they were inexplicable to me. I suspected her then of leading another life which she hid from me – but of course it was only the life which she had always led, filled with trivial routines and small pleasures. She would come back from tea with one of her childhood friends, her face quite bright with pleasure.

'Whom have you seen, my dear?' I would ask her.

'Oh, no one, Oscar, no one you know.'

But she could not refrain from describing to me then where she had been and what had been said. I listened always, but it is possible she suspected me of mocking her secretly, for often she would falter and fall silent. Now I am reminded of how I watched her with fascination whenever she was engaged in small household tasks – and how, if she saw me observing her, she would grow self-conscious and hesitant in her movements. It is as if I am describing a stranger, is it not? Perhaps I did not know Constance at all.

Nevertheless I am convinced that in our first years we were happy. It was only after the birth of our children that we grew more reserved towards each other. When she bore our first son, the sight of her with child repelled me somewhat: it is charming in religious art, but not elsewhere. I averted my eyes, and I busied myself about trivial matters. And, when Cyril was born, Constance herself became less childlike. I wished her to remain as she had been when I first met her, but I could no more restrain the progress of her maturity than I could hasten my own. For she required of me then a love which I could not give her: but she had learned from me how to dissimulate her feelings, and grew more distant. And so by gradual degree that innocent and joyful love which I had conceived for her I gave instead to my children.

It is strange how from the wreck of the past I can rescue only the smallest things: there was a tiny milk-cart, I remember, which I gave to Cyril and, when he broke one of its little horses, I spent the entire afternoon piecing it together with glue. He would ride upon my back, and I would tell him that our destination was the stars. For some reason, Vyvyan always wept when I lifted him up, and I would comfort him with pastilles.

To know that they are living somewhere, and that I shall never see them again: I cannot speak of it. I could weep for them longer than Niobe, who wept for ever, and mourn more bitterly than Demeter ever did: their children were snatched from them by the gods. I pushed mine away by my own deeds.

I find it hard now even to look upon other children in the street: I have this peculiar fear that they are in danger from the cabs and the omnibuses. When I see a father pick up his child and carry him upon his shoulders, it is all I can do to restrain myself from pleading with him not to do so. I do not know why this should be: I do not comprehend, sometimes, the forms which suffering takes.

I think I have written somewhere that marriage is a sort of forcing house. Constance never really understood me: that was no doubt why I married her; but boredom and frustration can lead to desperation, and desperation brings strange sins to fruit. I spent less and less of my time in Tite Street, and deception became necessary – but I cannot speak of my sins yet. I will employ what Pater calls the 'marvellous tact of omission'.

The marriage, then, was not satisfactory for either party. Sometimes, towards the end, it seemed to me that Constance and I were like characters out of *Modern Love*. I do not suppose that

78

anyone had experienced marital discord until Meredith invented it, but nevertheless it was a ridiculous posture – to be reduced to a poem. Even my mother was strangely affected; she would write letters to me explaining how sorrowful and lonely Constance was becoming and then, in my guilt, I would try to rekindle that love which, in Ovid's words, 'lights up the house'. And there were days when we were happy again but petty quarrels, and the shadow which my own life was beginning to cast, destroyed that happiness. It was as trite as a Drury Lane melodrama and yet wearying also, terribly wearying.

I have remembered one of the songs Constance and I played together in Tite Street:

> And never sit down with a tear or a frown
> But paddle your own canoe.

It is wonderfully suggestive, is it not?

7 September 1900

In the first years of marriage, my greatest fear was of poverty. Constance had a small income but that barely covered ordinary household expenses; money is rather like companionship – when one has it, one hardly thinks of it and, when one does not, one thinks of nothing else. It was only in this state of extreme need that I turned to journalism – I cannot imagine any other reason for doing so. I wrote criticism for the *Pall Mall Gazette* and other newspapers: I have always written quickly, with the fluency of the artist who has nothing whatever to say, and of course I never took my own criticism seriously, although I believe others did. It was astonishing to me how the latest novel, or the most recent volume of verse, could become such a matter of contention. I could find in them material only for humour. Modern English writing is not of great importance: bad work is always over-rated and good work is never understood. That is all. But is absurd to discuss such matters with the public: you can convince a fool of anything except his own folly.

Life is a very complex thing. There are those who, like Medusa, long for death and are granted eternal life instead; and there are those who, like Endymion, desire life and are frozen in endless sleep. It was much the case with me: I wished to do immortal work, and was offered the editorship of *Woman's World*. My wife urged me to take the post, while my friends merely laughed at it. And so, assailed on all sides, I amazed London with my self-sacrifice and became an editor.

Indeed it gave me the position in society which I had been in danger of losing. I was no longer the marvellous boy of my aesthetic period and I had not yet written the work which was to astonish my contemporaries. My editorship granted me, once more, a certain note of predominance. I commissioned, from influential ladies, articles on the effect of morals upon fabrics, or fabrics upon morals, I cannot remember which. I demonstrated conclusively that there was indeed life after Rider Haggard and *Lippincott's*, and that women could write more interestingly than men on the really important topics of civilisation: dress, food and furniture.

It was only when I joined the magazine, however, that I experienced the rigours of daily life. I would rise early to kiss the pink fingers of dawn immortalised by Marie Corelli, eat a substantial breakfast, discuss the news of the day with the children, and then walk in state down the King's Road. It is a drab little thoroughfare – an Oxford Street which is all street and no Oxford – but it leads unerringly to Sloane Square and the fiery-coloured world of the underground railway. The journey from Sloane Square to Charing Cross was endlessly fascinating for me: never have I been so close to the middle-classes, and I watched them intently for signs of life. Alas, I was disappointed.

Office life was strangely interesting: it was as if I had become part of a large family consisting almost entirely of mad aunts, and nephews who did not know how to spell. As an editor, it was my duty to be as interested in certain matters as others were – the correction of proofs, for example, which would have been better left to die unaided – and the rigours of my post exhausted me. The events of each day were exact and unvarying.

'Mr Wilde is in,' the office secretary would say as soon as I arrived, despite the fact that I was often alone with him in the room.

'Yes, Mr Cardew, I am in.'

'It is a little milder today, I think, Mr Wilde.'

'Yes, I felt it quite distinctly, Mr Cardew.'

'And are you well, Mr Wilde?'

'I am perfectly well, Mr Cardew. My wife is well, and my children are well also.'

'I am pleased to hear it.'

'Is there any urgent correspondence, Mr Cardew?'

He would hand me a number of letters. I would open them at once, while standing beside his desk – a habit which he detested, I believe, but I can never resist a sealed envelope. I must attack it at once.

'There seems to be nothing here of any importance, Mr Cardew.'

'Shall I reply to them in the customary manner?'

'That is a delightful idea, Mr Cardew.' I wonder what happened to Cardew?

I was bored with my life, then, but nevertheless office existence lent a form to my days which otherwise they would have lacked. I felt myself as an artist quite dead: the brilliant future which everyone had anticipated for me seemed already behind me.

And so my days passed, with the drama of my imagination reserved only for my correspondence. I did no serious work for the first three years of my marriage, except for the writing of my fairy stories – and I owe the inspiration for those entirely to my children. The nursery is the proper home of melodrama and I used to tell Vyvyan and Cyril stories of the Irish fairies – of the old woman who lived in the valley near our home in Moytura. She had stayed with the fairies for seven years. When she came home, she had no toes: she had worn them out in her wanderings after the little people. Cyril would sit wide-eyed in his bed when I told him of the leprechaun, the little shoe-maker, who repaired the fairies' shoes after they had finished their passionate dancing.

Sometimes I would tell them my own stories. They were about the love which is stronger than death, although it too must die, but they were of so perfect a shape that there was no sorrow within them, only a fiery joy. There was pain, but I placed the pain where no one would notice it. The boys were too young to understand, of course – and I believe I was also.

William Yeats came one year to spend Christmas with us and that willowy, awkward young man's face changed utterly when he spoke of faery things. He entranced the children with stories of the Fear-Gorta and the Water-Sheerie, of the little people who drink the new milk of the cows and the tall, white-armed women who come out of the air and crown themselves with roses and with lilies. Then, much to Cyril's amusement, he stood up and imitated their slow, dream-like walk.

By now William had roused himself to a pitch of excitement and, after Constance and the children had left the room, he talked animatedly to me of the Great Secret: Irishmen are always interested in secrets for we have been forced, too long, to live among the obvious. I knew of such things from the work of Eliphas Levi, but I did not wish to disillusion him. When the Sun has entered the Ram and before he has passed the Lion, there is a moment which trembles with the Song of the Immortal Powers – I remember Yeats leaning forward to touch me – and whoever listens to that song will become like the Immortal Powers themselves. I do not think, however, that they will sing to me. I must stop now: my cigarette has made me feel quite dizzy.

9 September 1900

I have another story. There was once a young prince, soon to become king of a great land and so powerful that his courtiers did not allow him to leave his palace. 'There is nothing there to interest your Highness,' said the Lord Chamberlain, 'only your subjects.' The young prince's tutor, who agreed on principle with everything the Lord Chamberlain said, explained to him that all the authorities disparaged travel as a way of seeing the world.

This tutor also had very advanced ideas about education, and the young prince's room, which was at the top of the highest tower of the palace, had nothing within it which was not beautiful or harmonious. The floor was of porphyry polished to the brightness of a star, and across it had been placed carpets from Tartary and rugs woven with pearls taken from the silent floors of the Indian Sea. Alabaster pillars curiously engraved, and furnishings made of the green stone which is to be found in Egyptian tombs, completed the effect. In the young prince's chamber, also, were the most beautiful objects in the world – a statue of Apollo so finely wrought that it seemed to move in the changing light, a tapestry woven from the finest silk which pictured the true history of Endymion – who slept not out of enchantment but because he feared old age. There were great Venetian paintings hanging on the walls, which in their subtle tints and shades turned the smoke of battle into a mist and great armies into the figures of a reverie; and, in a little book-case made of ivory taken from the unicorn, were to be found the first editions of perfect sonnets, of so intricate a structure and such purity of diction that all who read them felt themselves in love.

All these exquisite objects the young prince contemplated with wonder: he would gaze for hours at the tapestry of Endymion and marvel at the mystery of Beauty which grows more sacred in sleep, and he would gently touch the figure of Apollo as a blind man might touch the lips of his beloved; sometimes he would read the sonnets of love and feel the holy breath of the poet upon his face.

And yet the most wonderful effect in this room of wonderful things was the window through which the young prince could look down upon his kingdom; it was made not of glass but of precious stones, a blend of sardonyx, chrysoberyl and azerodrach which had been fused together over a period of many years. It was such a window that all who looked through it saw objects brighter than the day and yet the subtle comingling of jewels gave out a mysterious light in which the seasons never changed: there was no gleam of frost here and no harshness of sunlight. Day followed night on quiet feet, and the shadows were like the bruise which touches a peach. 'We cannot,' said the tutor, 'allow His Highness to be affected by worldly things. If he heard that the seasons change, he would lose all confidence in his own authority.' And, as always, the Lord Chamberlain agreed with the tutor.

And so the boy who was to become king spent many hours gazing out of this wonderful window. He could see the ornamental gardens of the palace where storks cried and flowers sang – and, behind the gardens, he could see the jade-green fields of his dominion. Spring fled from summer and autumn bowed its head before winter, but it was always quiet here, the light so calm and clear that the young prince would often fall into a gentle sleep.

And then one day – it was his thirteenth birthday – he fell asleep and dreamed a strange dream. He was taken from his chamber by a masked guide and led into the streets of a great city; he suddenly found himself alone, in a mean alley where a lonely boy was writing 'I am' upon a wall. Here were children in rags, huddled together for warmth. An old man begged for coins and was scoffed at by all those who passed. A young woman screamed for help and found none. 'This,' his guide said, 'is Poverty and Sorrow. Learn of them.'

When the young prince awoke, he was afraid for he did not understand what he had seen. And so he called for his Lord Chamberlain and his tutor, and he questioned them: 'What are these things I have dreamed of, Poverty and Sorrow?' The courtiers were quite astounded, since they could not imagine how he had discovered such things in his beautiful chamber. 'They are vulgarisms, your Highness,' the Lord Chamberlain replied, 'invented by the common people. They are not known in Society.'

'They are simply words,' the tutor said, 'but they have been quite disproven by the best philosophers and artists.' The young prince, although much troubled, accepted their answers and returned to his violet couch by the window: he watched the fruits of his garden blossoming and falling untasted, and he saw the flowers give out their scent and, in the evening, hide their faces.

And then he dreamed again. This is what he dreamed. His guide took him from his palace and into the streets of a great city. He found himself in a mean alley but it was evening now, and harsh lights cast strange shadows. Young men jostled each other and made much noise, and young girls were involved in curious games with cards and pebbles. There were men and women who danced together on a rough stone floor to the sound of rude instruments, and there were others who sat together in dark corners whispering. There was laughter, and wine was spilt upon the ground. 'This is Passion and Joy,' the guide said. 'Learn of them.'

And, when the young prince awoke, he was filled with a strange fear and he called out to the Lord Chamberlain and his tutor. 'What are Passion and Joy?' he asked them. 'For I have seen such things as these and they have troubled me.' And the courtiers were astonished, 'They are curious, savage words, your Highness,' the tutor told him. 'They have not been used in polite speech for many years.' 'They are not known in Society,' the Lord Chamberlain added, 'I have been a member of it for sixty years and to my recollection they have never once been mentioned.'

But the young prince was troubled still. And he went to his window and gazed out at the beautiful, unchanging world which it fashioned for him. And then he saw what he had never seen before: in the distance, across one of the verdigris meadows, a troupe of jugglers and dancers rode by on horses and, in the window's precious light, they seemed clearer than the images in his dreams. They were to perform that evening in the great city, but of course the prince knew nothing of that. But he heard their shouts and their laughter, and they reminded him of his dreams. The young prince waved and called to them but they were engaged in quarrelling among themselves and could not hear him. And then the young prince beat his fists against the window which had the fragility of all beautiful things, in order that they might notice him. But by now the troupe of circus people had passed over the horizon.

And the young prince was mournful. The beautiful paintings in his room no longer seemed beautiful to him, Endymion was lifeless merely, and the intricate statue of Apollo a made thing, a fabrication. The books also displeased him for they did not contain the words Passion or Joy, or the words Pain and Sorrow. And the elaborate furnishings of his chamber oppressed the prince; they weighed heavily upon his spirits and he could no longer sleep. Each morning he gazed out of the window to see if the troupe might return and, when they did not come, each day the young prince grew paler and more fretful.

His courtiers grew worried. 'It is quite obvious to me,' said the tutor to the Lord Chamberlain, 'that it is the strain of the bills and proclamations which you give him to sign.' 'I blame it all upon the lessons in mathematics which you insist on giving him,' the Lord Chamberlain replied. 'They have made him quite unwell.' Of course the young prince heard nothing of this because the courtiers never spoke in his presence unless he spoke to them first. But the prince had nothing to say now.

He grew worse as the days passed; and then, on the seventh day, at the end of the city's festivities, the circus people passed through the malachite fields once more in order to return to their own country. The prince saw them, and his joy was so great that he could not contain it. He waved and cried to them – 'please stop, please come to me, with your bright harnesses and your coloured robes!' – but they could not hear him, and they continued riding. In desperation, the prince took the statue of Apollo and hurled it through the window of jewels. 'Wait for me!' he called. 'I am coming!' But already they had travelled far into the distance, and not one of them looked back at the palace, which was known as Sans Souci.

And then the prince experienced a sorrow greater than any he had felt in his dreams, and a pain more terrible than any which the guide had shown to him. He found a jagged splinter from the window of sardonyx and chrysoberyl and, finding his breast beneath his richly woven doublet, plunged the jewel into his heart.

The circus troupe heard a faint noise in the distance. 'What was that?' one minstrel asked the dwarf who rode beside him. 'It sounded like a glass breaking, or perhaps a wave crashing against a shore,' the dwarf replied. 'You are too absurd,' and the minstrel laughed, and the troupe rode on.

10 September 1900

In the few years before I went to prison, I became a symbol of that Society which sent me there in scorn. From my Oxford days I had been accepted everywhere, but as an ornament merely. It was not until after I had left the *Woman's World* and begun my brilliant series of books and plays that I became the leading figure in the pageant which the really powerful people in England wished to create. For all of my drama was, to those who had eyes but not ears, a social event. In my earlier years, my mission had been to bring art into life and in drama I discovered that the two become perfect in combination. I should have made the audience perfect, also, as I realise now to my cost.

I was never performed at the advanced theatres, at the Independent or the New Century – that would have been sheer indulgence on my part – for I was as much a landmark of the West End as the Savoy Hotel. Of course I knew that my plays were potboilers – exquisite potboilers – and I disowned each one as soon as it was successful: if one had failed, I would have hugged it to myself and proclaimed it the true voice of my art.

My first nights were as carefully planned as my productions: in the little theatre in King Street, the young men wore green carnations, that sweet arsenic flower which is the emblem of a doomed life, and the women wore lilies which perfumed the whole of London. The Prince would come, and with him the whole of the fashionable world. Only the critics felt out of place.

I was extravagant: I used to say that the only way to waste money was to save it and it was only when I entered the Bankruptcy Court in convict dress that I had to count the true cost of my profligacy – a cost which was not to be reckoned in coin alone. I dressed like a Celt rather than an Englishman. My buttonhole cost me 10/6, and, like all expensive things, it expired at once; it became my fancy to purchase a new article of clothing each day – I was a saint collecting my own relics. Dress is the most complete representation of modern civilisation, after all, and I sailed through life on cloth like Faust upon his mantle.

Like a Celt, also, I built castles of gold which I would then enter. I hired a hansom which followed me on a retainer and, in flight from domestic life, I lived in restaurants, hotels and private rooms. I would sit in the Café Royal and discuss improbable things, and dine at Willis's with impossible people. I was vain and the world loved my vanity. If the English can be said to admire anything, they admire success, and I became the object of imitation upon the stage and in the popular press. I had in those brilliant years the over-brightness of Pico della Mirandola and I thought that I, like him, lived in a time of hyacinths.

I spoke on equal terms with princes and with duchesses. I paid visits to them in the country and dined with them in London. I was the distinguished equivalent of a Saturday Popular Concert and I suppose that, in the modern phrase, I 'sang for my supper'. They permitted me into their drawing rooms because I brought their own illusions to brilliant life. At dinner parties and at receptions, in salons and in cafés, I was surrounded by those who dominated life: I did not flatter them, but I understood them for I, too, believed in the value of appearances. I sustained the over-dressed with my wit and the under-educated by my paradoxes. I held their own fantasies to the light of my conversation and they shone. But they did so only because they were quite transparent. Only when I was put on trial for immorality did the English recognise this, and then they stamped upon me with all the fury of those who have betrayed themselves.

My conversation was immaculate – I turned it into an art in which the most important things were left unsaid. But I did not disillusion those who listened to me, and there lay the most serious flaw in my character. I enjoyed praise, I admit it. I like to be liked. And my true fault was not that I succumbed to strange sins or mingled in worthless company, but that I craved fame and success even when I knew them to be fraudulent. And so I made a philosophy out of insincerity which was universally admired. I proclaimed that insincerity represented the multiplicity of the personality.

But I do not miss the company of those who glittered with jewels and with the colours of the mocking bird. I feel utterly alone now because of the absence of those real friends whom I possessed during that period. With the rich and the powerful I never felt wholly at ease – my performances for them sometimes wearied me and left me terribly empty. It was the same with other writers: I was too much ahead of them to be comfortable in their company. It was only with those who accepted me entirely that I could take off the mask of the carnival and enjoy the sweet comfort of conversation shared.

Ada Leverson was my dearest friend in London. I called her 'the Sphinx' because of the indecipherable messages she left for me and often, at a very late hour, I would visit her little house near Gloucester Road. She had a habit of being discovered doing something useful, like reading German aloud. But I would always ignore it.

'Ah, Sphinx, I see this is your leisure hour. I am delighted to catch you at home.'

'I rarely go out after midnight, Oscar.'

'That is so sensible of you, Sphinx. You should only be seen in the tawny-faced sunlight, when men will stop and wonder at your beauty.'

'I am afraid they will only wonder where it has gone. Do have a drink, Oscar.'

'Where is your husband? Have you hidden him?'

'Ernest is asleep.'

'Asleep? After midnight? I am surprised at you, Sphinx, for indulging him.'

'You must have been with very dull people tonight, Oscar. You are talking nonsense.'

'I have been dining with Lord Stanhope. Really, he is nothing more than an exaggerated farmer. He insisted that I discuss Tennyson with him while we were going in to dinner.'

'You know you adore Tennyson, Oscar, although I have always thought of him as the Sidney Colvin of literature.'

'Never speak disrespectfully of Sidney Colvin. It shows a maturity in excess of your years.'

'I am always excessive. Did Constance tell you that I went shopping with her this afternoon?'

'With my money and your taste, she must have worked miracles.'

'She seemed rather distracted. I had to warn her twice against buying corded silk.'

'Yes, I have often mentioned corded silk to her myself. But you said she was distracted. About what?'

'You know perfectly well. She says she hardly sees you. And she found Arthur removing three empty bottles of champagne from your bedroom –'

'What else does one do with empty bottles?'

'And she says your mother complains that you never visit her. I am sorry to talk to you like this, Oscar, but really I am the only one who will.'

'I know, dear Sphinx, and I sit here contrite. Where is that drink you foolishly promised me? I suppose I will have to fetch it myself.'

'Tread quietly, Oscar. The servants are below you.'

'I was amusing about servants tonight. I said I have always been fond of them: without them, no dinner party is complete. Do you like that?'

'It is a little below your best, but it will serve.'

'That is very amusing. Did I tell you about my new story? I have called it "The Double Beheading". I have no theme as yet, but the title is delightful don't you think?'

And so we would talk together, until one or both of us had tired. 'Already, Sphinx,' I would say then, 'I can hear the horses of Apollo pawing impatiently at the gates. I must leave you and dear, sleeping Ernest.'

'Ah yes, the importance of being Ernest.'

'It is a little below your best, Sphinx, but it will serve.' And then I would return to Tite Street, and lie awake upon my bed until dawn.

And yet now, when I look back upon those evenings and search my past for traces of that love and humility which must now be my guides, I do not find it there, in the companionship of those I loved and who loved me. I am not sure that even with them I was not playing a part. I was so much the master of my period that I knew how to adopt effortlessly all its disguises. But I think also that I was – or thought myself to be – so much the lord of life that I was able to take on whatever character that was required and remain apart. I took off one mask only to reveal another. I imagined that the world was mine; that there was nothing which I could not do. A fierce joy consumed me. I was free.

But in truth there was no real liberty for me. I was imprisoned by my success just as if I had been caught in a house of mirrors where, turning quickly about myself, I saw only my own image. For I had become a spectacle merely and often, at night, I would sit alone in Tite Street trying to see things coolly and calmly. I knew then, in the dead hours, what I had become.

But if I found my own Gethsemane in the dark night of London, I was in other ways quite the opposite of Christ. The thorns tore at the divine temples, but eternal flowers blossomed in His heart because it was full of love. My own head was crowned with myrtles and with vine-leaves, but my heart expired beneath the poisoned dart of the world. In my plays I had made light of all the things that were dearest to me; in my life I had betrayed all those who were closest to me. I was the Juggernaut, heaped with flowers, which crushes all those who come near to it.

Now, when those who have loved or admired me have left my side, I do not truly know who I am. I have survived the disaster, but I have emerged from the wreckage as dazzled and as bereft of thought as a child emerging from the womb. I catch myself now, in my loneliness, empty of action and of imagination. I can spend minutes, hours even, staring out of the small window which looks upon the courtyard, staring at nothing, thinking of nothing.

Could it be that I, who have written so much about the powers of the personality, do not – after everything which has happened to me – know what my own personality is? That would be the tragedy of my life, if tragedy were to be found anywhere within it. I can say only one thing truly: in that strange complicity between the world and the individual character, I was one in whom the world played the largest part. My greatest efforts can be traced to the love of praise, my greatest catastrophes to the love of pleasure.

Of course that is why I have always been enchanted by the lives of anchorites, for the true artist is always looking for that hooded figure who is 'the opposite of himself'. I consulted the authorities on the lives of the saints – Flaubert and Villiers de L'Isle Adam – and I even began a story of my own upon that theme. There are fragments of it among the notes I made in prison, but they were stolen at Dieppe. I believe the princess Myrrhina approaches the cave of the hermit, Honorius, to tempt him with her silks and perfumes. She tells him of sins and palaces, and he tells her of the love of God. She mocks at his rags, and he implores her to leave him. She murmurs to him of subtle foods and sweet drinks which, once taken, grant you the memories of the world and then in scorn she scatters his coarse bread and his cup of brackish water. And he is tempted. I have done no further work upon it, but I had an ending in mind which I have yet to write down.

Myrrhina, in her arrogance, tempts Honorius to such effect that he embraces her and puts his mouth to her mouth – I want the music of cymbals here – but the punishment of God is a mysterious thing. In that act of surrender Honorius expires, and his embrace is so passionate that Myrrhina cannot free herself. As he grows cold in death, his arms tighten around her like the root of an ancient tree. And she looks with horror upon that body which in her pride she lured into sin: she sees that body decay even as it imprisons her in the fatal embrace. And Myrrhina, too, dies. Is that not a charming ending?

There is, after all, a strange justice in the workings of fate: we cry out against it at first but then it whispers to us the secrets of our soul and we bow our head in silence. I realise now that my social and financial success would have destroyed me, more completely and terribly, than my disaster if they had continued. The artist within me was dying, and had to enter a prison before he could be reborn. In the days of triumph I was like a large goldfish which has choked from devouring too much bread. The meal did not nourish me: it simply distended my stomach.

And in truth I became fat – bloated almost. I drank too much, far too much, so that I might retain the intoxication of spirit which propelled me forward. My wife was dismayed – and even my little sons turned away from me. My family said nothing but, just as I saw little of them, they were in turn pleased to see little of me. My friends – my real friends, not those who surrounded me and held me up for others to gape at – tried to warn me that I was losing myself in a mist of excess. I remember one conversation with Shaw, in the Café Royal, where he took me to one side and spoke quietly and seriously to me of the way my life was going. I remember him saying to me, 'You are betraying us, us Irishmen.' And I laughed in his face. I could not take him seriously. And then he told me to read again one of my own stories, 'The Fisherman and His Soul', and how I had written that no life can bloom if there is no love to nourish it. Naturally, I paid no attention.

There were other intimations, also. At the time of my greatest success, I was suspected of the greatest infamies. My own writing – and my plays especially – contained evidence of those disclosures which I most feared. But England is the home of Tartuffe and, as long as I amused the English, they chose to ignore the whisperings which were then circulating about my private life. But I, too, had been infected by the same hypocrisy – my work will show what my secret voice continually murmured to me, that my life was hollow and my triumphs fraudulent.

12 September 1900

I was this morning looking through my edition of Landor's *Imaginary Conversations of Literary Men and Statesmen*, for reasons which now escape me, and there, in the chapter devoted to Porson and Southey, I discovered some of my newspaper cuttings. It is not my custom to keep such things but I may have placed them there as an addition to Landor's collection. Most of them were to no account, but something from the *San Francisco Tribune* pleased me:

HE HAS COME: OSCAR WILDE, THE FAMOUS AESTHETE, arrived on the Pioneer Train yesterday morning. The notorious poet and sunflower addict has come to spread the gospel of BEAUTY through our benighted community. He is six feet and two inches tall, has a large head and man-size hands. When asked if he could acquit himself in man-to-man combat he replied he was ready for the noble art as long as our men did not play by the Queensberry rules. When asked his age, he said twenty-seven or thereabouts but he had no memory for unimportant dates. He told your reporter that he has come to lecture on the HOUSE BEAUTIFUL. When asked about the MINE BEAUTIFUL, he replied what is Mine is yours, treating us to a specimen of that wit for which he has become famous all over our country . . .

I cannot go on although, alas, the reporter did. Here is another cutting, from the *Pall Mall Gazette* of 1893:

Mr Oscar Wilde tells us that he is about to write a new play. When asked what the subject might be, he replied that it would be a drama of modern married life. Mr Wilde has changed with the years. He is no longer the dashing aesthete of former times. When asked about his present life, he talked about his wife and sons with the utmost gravity. We are pleased to see this change in Mr Wilde, who has disproved reports that he is a genius *mal entendu* and has now condescended to grace the English stage with more fruits from his pen . . .

It is extraordinary the number of clichés which can be hurled into one sentence. I have found something from the *Woman's Age* of the same year:

We were privileged to be granted an interview with Mr Wilde before the opening night of his new play, *A Woman of No Importance*. Mr Wilde entered the smoking room of his charming house in Chelsea and greeted us warmly. He is a tall, broad man with a large and clean-shaven face. He has a heavy jaw and thick lips, but his hair is carefully waved and his eyes are deep and expressive. He was fashionably dressed, wearing a black frock-coat, light-coloured trousers, a brightly flowered waistcoat and a white silk cravat which was fastened with an amethyst pin. 'I would have brought my cane,' he told us, 'but my son has hidden it. He has a great respect for what is beautiful.' Mr Wilde has a curious manner of talking, a kind of sing-song voice in which he accentuates the wrong syllables in the sentence. . . .

It is wonderful how journalists have an eye only for the obvious. To bring my life quite 'up to date', here is something from the *Gazette* of 1895:

Oscar Wilde, the so-called gentleman, is to bring a case against the Marquess of Queensberry for defaming his character. We do not presume to judge of this affair before its culmination in the courts, but suffice it to be said that Wilde's conduct, no doubt befitting of a so-called artist, has given rise to scandalous rumours which it will be in his interest to dispel. We are not of the party which seeks to find the worst wherever they look, but it is time that modern morals were placed in the light of public gaze and judged for what they are. . . .

An interesting collection.

14 September 1900

Maurice is going to Switzerland with More Adey: I have warned
him in the past about the unpredictability of the northern races,
but he pretends not to understand me. I shall miss him. I tire
easily now. I find it difficult to write for long periods and Maurice
has a charming hand. When he returns I shall ask him to take
dictation. If he can survive Switzerland, he can survive anything.

I was speaking, was I not, of the days of my great success? The
voice of fatality was there always, even though I took care not to
listen to it. But the presence of doom colours with a darker shade
even one's most fiery moments, and I saw through my own
attitudes as if they were shadows thrown upon a screen. Modern
aesthetics, after all, is only an extension of modern morality – both
of them conceal the truth and the shame that comes from
knowledge of the truth. When I was a boy I was always angered by
the hypocrisy of my elders – but could I not be accused of that sin?
Does one come to be the thing one most despises?

For what did I, who should have been a great poet, what did I
become? I became a symbol of modern society, both in its rise and
in its fall. Yet in order to become a symbol, one must know
thoroughly what one represents: self-consciousness is the essence
of success. And here lay the hypocrisy for I knew very well, as
Pater did, that I lived in a worn-out society, theatrical in its art,
theatrical in its life, theatrical even in its piety. But I could no
more escape from my period than a bird can fly without wings. I
sought for visible rather than intellectual success; I wrote quickly
and without thought; I mimicked the pleasures of the age and
made light of its pains. Like Augustine, in that terrible phrase,
'factus sum mihi regio egestatis'.

I knew also, even when expounding my philosophy in a phrase,
even when I stood in the drawing rooms of London, that I was of
an alien race. And those who invited me knew it, too. They

laughed at me behind my back, and I became more irridescent. They were baffled by me, and so I made my paradoxes more brilliant still. I did not talk to them: I addressed them. It is possible, I suppose, that I was a little frightened of them.

For I was always, essentially, a foreigner among them, a civilised man trying to break down the walls of the barbarians. I was Irish, and therefore in permanent exile. As a Celt, I was part of a proud race with a native quickness and imagination which the English have never possessed. I spring from the race of Swift and Sheridan. O'Connell and Parnell came before me, Irishmen destroyed by scandal – it is the one revenge which the English have fashioned into an art. I was a devotee of Greek love, which marked me out more brutally than I then knew. And, through it all, the scarlet thread of illegitimacy runs: but it was not Ariadne's thread, for it led me only further into the labyrinth.

Outcasts, since they dwell in the shadows, learn to recognise each other by small signs and movements. I had always, for example, been interested in the criminal classes even before I became a member of them. In prison, I came to enjoy their company: they sought fresh sensations, as I did. And I was fascinated by them also because they were ahead of me and could teach me. They had found a delightful combination: they possessed the easy manner of the rich and the vices of the poor.

Naturally I understood the anarchists – like John Barlas. I admired him: he was a foolish man, but a necessary one. Power seems to me so fearful a thing that my instincts were entirely with those who wished to subvert it, who tore off the gaudy raiment and pointed to the skeleton beneath. Of course Nihilists have monstrously flawed characters, but just as imaginative fire can visit the disturbed mind and bruised soul of a poet such as Dowson, so the rage against the established order is beautiful in itself, whatever form it chooses to take.

But the poor are truly the outcasts of the world. One has only to walk down a London street to see the suffering. It is one long chaplet of sorrowful mysteries. The unseen host of the poor bear the marks of our civilisation like scars; that is why the middle class never look at them. It would be to examine the wounds which they themselves have inflicted. The deed is done, but the consequences must be shunned. I believe I explained in *The Soul of Man under Socialism* that my interest in poverty was aesthetic primarily – I desired only that ugliness and squalor should be removed. I am what is known as a speculative radical, and I have a positive distaste for Fabianism and philanthropy – they are cures for civilisation far more deadly than its diseases. But now I believe that we are creating, in the poor, a society which will wreak a terrible vengeance on our own. I have always been convinced that our civilisation has the transparency and evanescence of a bubble floating, in that charming manner which bubbles have, before being blown away in the wind.

In one of my stories the young king thought only of his magnificent robes, until he saw the small children who wove the silk for them; he marvelled at his magnificent jewels, until he saw those who died in order to find them. It is a mysterious truth, but then sorrow is always mysterious; the paper which I write on now, the clothes I am wearing, the bed upon which I sleep: they have all been made by the toil of others, created out of the indigence and the suffering of the poor. I am lying on the poor. I am writing with them. They are my food and my drink. I see their pain everywhere, like paint.

It is my privilege – I understand this now – to have become like them, to have become a byword for infamy, an indigent wanderer who must beg for his bread. And yet I believe my destiny to be more terrible than theirs. Yeats has called one of his stories 'The Crucifixion of an Outcast', and in that story he writes of me. He writes of one who, on the road to his crucifixion, sang and told wonderful stories; yet his accusers showed him no mercy because of that, but hated him all the more fiercely for awakening forgotten longings in their breasts. Even under the shadow of the cross, they despised him for showing to them the beauty and the mystery of the world. And, in the end, even the beggars left him, crucified, to the mercy of wild beasts. Even the outcasts turned against the outcast.

And now I must write to Maurice, warning him against the views.

15 September 1900

Wherever I run, I cannot find peace. Yesterday evening the pain in my ear abated, and I decided to celebrate on the boulevards. I went with a few acquaintances to a little restaurant near the Madeleine; almost as soon as I had entered the door the proprietor, with many expressions of rather fulsome regret, asked me to leave. It seemed that my presence had startled some English tourists. I looked at them and bowed, and they turned their heads away; I feel sure they came from Bayswater. They always do. Of course I left the restaurant although my companions, of a more phlegmatic temperament than my own, stayed. Contrary to popular belief, I shrink from confrontations of such a kind. I seek the night, like the Hamadryades, but only to hide myself.

My companions, I admit it, were two or three of the boys I know here. Although I cannot shower gold upon them – I am no longer mythological – I can on occasions produce banknotes. My favourites, Eugène and Léon, will stand by me in anything except adversity – their age has taught them wisdom. Eugène is sixteen, and he has the eyes of Antinous; he is the protector of a younger boy who sells matches. At least I have not seen him without matches, but I believe he gives them away to tourists of the Socratic kind who smile upon him. Léon haunts the cafés, although he has never been known to eat or drink in them.

It is fitting perhaps that I, who sought youth and the pleasures of youth, now have no friends of my own age. Indeed even those who have been closest to me – Bobbie Ross, Bosie, Reggie Turner – have always been much younger than myself. I feel more at ease with them because I need to make no definite impression. With people like Frank Harris or W. E. Henley, conversation was a kind of rugby football – I was continually forced to strike attitudes, and defend myself. Where I sought friendship and beauty they desired competitors and the struggle in the dust. And so I shunned them. Now, ancient and alone, I have become a monument to another era.

My friends in England telegraph me to say that I can begin my life anew, that like the old man in Anatole France's fable I can still add 'a new wing to the building'. I have told myself the same thing in the past – that my recent experience would create in me a new and deeper art, that the personality is changed by suffering as an iron glows when it is placed in the fire. But such hopes are illusions. The appetites and aspirations of man are endless but, alas, the experience is confined. The tragedy of my life is that my growth has been arrested – I trudge round and round the circle of my personality. It is as if I had been condemned to haunt the scenes of my crimes and frighten those who came near to me. The places are the same; the boys are the same.

I am not Rabelaisian. I find it difficult now to write about my vices. And yet I wrote once to Bosie that a man's highest moment comes when he kneels in the dust and tells the sins of his life. I must now tell mine. I have of course no models on which to draw for inspiration. Baudelaire wished to interest heaven and hell in his sins and, since he did not write at length, he may have succeeded. I cannot perform such miracles: I cannot turn the mire to silver, or the white stains to gold. I can provide only this chronicle which in confusion I set down. I must do like the Romans – take my entrails in my hands, and die twice over.

I first experienced the pleasures of Greek love with Harry Marriller. Before that I had glimpses merely – from Lord Ronald Gower, that strange carved figure, and from the dark streets of great cities. But then it seemed to me to be a carnival for which I had not found the appropriate mask, and I let it pass by with its strange scents and purple music. And then I met Harry. I had known him when he was a boy: he used to live in Thames House where Frank Miles and I had found lodgings on leaving Oxford. Quite unexpectedly, he wrote to me one day at Tite Street. I remember the year precisely, for it was the year in which Cyril was born: 1885. I was thirty-one, and Harry was twenty. It was a perfectly delightful letter and in my reply I asked him to visit us in Chelsea. I believe that even then the weight of domestic life was becoming burdensome to me.

Harry came and dined with us. He was an agreeable boy, with that fondness for romantic poetry which only the young possess.

101

He was at Cambridge still, and we talked of Plato and the fiery visions of Heraclitus. Constance left the table – she grew easily tired then – and I remember quite well the nervousness I felt when I was alone with Harry. We drank heavily, and I believe I said marvellous things about the *Symposium*. And then, with the spell of Greek words around us, I put a hand on Harry's arm and he did not resist. I experienced then for the first time that passion which was to haunt me and which I was to pursue through the folly of my years – that weakening of the body and that heightening of sensation which leaves one the prey solely of appetite.

The intimacies which passed between us were schoolboyish, and yet they awakened in me both a fierce joy and a terrible shame. I resolved that I would not see him again – and, indeed, after that night we exchanged letters but not confidences. He had opened my eyes, however, and awakened in me a nature which had previously lain dormant. I had known that physical beauty is not the property of any one sex but hovers above both like the *putti* in the paintings of Fra Angelico, but I had thought such beauty to be merely an abstraction – I had not understood that it could be tasted and enjoyed without losing its savour. But, when I abjured the wonderful idealism of my art, I took the first step on the path which was to lead me into the wilderness. I had been sitting with Socrates, but now I had found Alcibiades on my other hand, and I took my meat, and drank my wine, with him.

A year passed, a year in which I fled from the nature that had been revealed to me. If I had hinted at the truth to Constance, I believe she would have turned from me in horror and contempt. And so I kept my secret, nursed it, nourished it with sighs and with groans. But the gods are cruel and play with us: I had gone on a pilgrimage to Oxford to visit Pater, and it was after I had attended one of his long exequies on the life of sensation without passion, that I fell for the second time.

For, after the lecture, a young student came up to me in the street and introduced himself. I see now that I have always been the seduced, not the seducer; although in popular imagination I now sit in the Inferno beside Gilles de Retz, I do not believe that I ever instigated the passions which were to consume me. The student, of course, was Robert Ross. His is a sweet character, with the sweetness of those without ambition, and in those days he had the quick responsiveness of a child. I liked him at once, and my first impressions are never wrong.

After we had met, I invited him to Tite Street and, in the months that followed, he became a regular visitor there. Robbie was amusing, and he had the gift of asking questions that only I could answer. He admired me, and so in his company I became admirable: in conversation with him, I was able to evolve some of my best dialogues. It is strange, is it not, how a person can adore one's soul so much that they adore one's body also? We were intimate with each other, but the passion in our friendship was only a passing thing. And indeed I was quite happy to allow the physical intimacies between us to lapse. I have never been for long attracted to those of my own class – it is to lie with oneself rather than with another. But Robbie had shown me the path, which then I trod willingly but, later, with ever more weary steps. It seemed to me, however, that Socratic love brought out the finest qualities in me; the imagination which had before been stifled, flourished and grew strong in its light. I grew to understand myself, and was greedy for further revelations.

Robbie introduced me to a circle of Uranians – More Adey, Maurice Schwabe, Reggie Turner. They were perfectly frank about their lives, and unfamiliar vistas were opened out to me: of ugly cast-iron urinals in the North of London, of parks where the red and blue of the soldiery might be glimpsed between the trees, of a skating rink in Knightsbridge where strange flowers blossomed upon the ice. I found it fascinating, but in those days I did not allow the new passion to control my life, as it did theirs. I preferred to immerse myself in their company rather than their crimes. We would visit the Crown public house in the Strand, or a scented bar in St James's, and consume the evening in drinks and cigarettes while strange, painted creatures walked past.

The Crown, like all Cities of the Plain, was a charming place from which to watch the world. There were boxing prints upon the wall, some of which appeared to be signed, and dark red shades which obscured the gas-light in an admirable manner. Young men with sporting papers and old men with cheroots gathered around the 'Marjeries', as they were called in a charmingly old-fashioned way, and laughed with them. I can still recall one young man who went by the name of Kitty Fisher; he walked the Strand and Fleet Street.

'I love my City gents,' he told me one evening, 'they're so regular. Are you a City man yourself, Mr Wilde?'

'No. I am a writer, my dear.'

'A writer, really? Well, that must be interesting. Would I have caught your name in the *News*?'

'No, my dear, I have not had that pleasure.' I ordered him a port.

'And what does a writer like yourself do of an evening, then? Would he like to feel Kitty's prickle by any chance?'

'No, my dear, I have already had *that* pleasure.'

'Oh, go on. I never forget a face, not of a handsome gentleman like yourself.'

And so the hours would pass. Nothing was serious there, and all that seemed to be serious was reduced to a mist of laughter. I remember that every public figure could, in their conversation, be turned to absurd caricature – Gladstone was referred to as Milady Gladstone and Rosebery known simply as 'the princess'; Sir Charles Dilke was, to his admirers, the 'empress of Chelsea'. This amused me, and it came also as something of a relief. Modern civilisation can only be endured when it is mocked, and the great and famous are quite impossible when they are placed on pedestals. I liked the notion that they could be brought down by humour. I was playing with fire, but it is the prettiest thing in the world to play with.

Through Robbie's friends, I met others. There were actors who frequented the same places, young men like Roland Atwood, Oswald Yorke and Sidney Barraclough who had decided that the life of the theatre was a perfect extension of their own rather dramatic sensibilities. And their company was charming to me, filled with a gaiety quite absent in the charnel house of journalism or the poisoned garden of professional literary men.

It was in the Crown that I met John Gray, a poet with a profile. I had dreamed, I think, of perfect Socratic companionship, of a life of love and art conducted on terms of equality. With Gray I believed it to be possible, but he made it clear to me that he did not like me 'in that way': it was an atrocious phrase to fall from the lips of a poet. Still, he graciously allowed me to pay for the publication of his first volume. For me, alas, the love of equals was to prove an idle dream. I, who aspired so high, both in art and in life, was doomed to be betrayed by my inferiors. It could not have been otherwise.

For even in those days, some years before my trial, I met certain of the young men who were to be implicated in my later sorrows: some of them because spectators only, but there were others who were to betray me and, through their betrayal, hasten the course of my downfall. Edward Shelley was one of those – a pale, tense young man but not without the beauty of those who suffer from quite imaginary anxieties. I met him at my publishers, where he worked as a clerk; he asked me to autograph one of my books, and so great was his embarrassment that he hardly dared to look at me as he did so. I felt for him both pity and affection – sentiments agreeable in themselves, but terribly dangerous in combination. But there has always been something in those who have no sense of their own worth which moves me.

When I gave Edward a seat at the first night of *Lady Windermere's Fan*, I had placed him beside the young French poet, Pierre Louys – with what paroxysms of embarrassment, Edward confessed to me later, did he sit there and make conversation with the young Frenchman. He was nervous precisely because he felt unworthy of his position as my friend: can anything be more ridiculous, or more piteous? It touches me still, even though later he betrayed me in the grossest manner. Indeed, he betrayed me three times – I will not draw the obvious parallel – once with lies to the private detectives whom Queensberry had hired to destroy me and twice when he committed perjury in the witness box at the Old Bailey.

All regret is quite useless – I, who have so much to regret, have learned that at least – but there was something in Edward Shelley's temperament which should have warned me, if I were of a character to be affected by warnings. For I noticed in him the weaknesses by which the Uranian temperament is marked – the guilt and hysteria which, in flawed characters like Edward's, follow always on passion with swift feet. After I had known him for some months, he would write appalling letters to me, accusing himself of sins which he had not the spirit to commit, and of self-betrayal when he was in reality betraying only me. When he involved me in domestic arguments with his father, to the extent that I was asked to bail him out from a police station in the suburbs after an assault, I should have sent him out of my life with a few stern but well-chosen words. I did not do so: well, in the memorable phrase of Arthur Pinero, I have 'learned my lesson'.

There was one boy who warned me of the dangers that I was courting – Peter Burford, who stood by me until the end and, in his nobility of character, refused to testify against me. I met him at the Alhambra, during one of those intervals which one finds so necessary at most theatrical productions. Constance was in the country, and I took him back with me to Tite Street. He was no stranger to the ways of lust but he had also a curious innocence which, because I had never possessed it, fascinated me. He was of course from a much lower station than myself – he worked as a carpenter in Grape Street – but he had a soundness of instinct which I was to find invaluable. I have never found it difficult to associate with those of an inferior position. Such matters are of no consequence to me. I am an Irishman. Indeed it is possible that the English grew to hate me only when I was revealed as a member of the only truly classless society in London, although I do not think it could be described as socialistic – some of the young men would have been quite happy to become duchesses. Two of them did.

Peter Burford and I became great friends. We would eat simple meals together at the Florence – all meals are simple there – and he would lecture me about the dangers of my life. He had a true appreciation of my genius, and as a result found several glaring faults in my character. I would accept his criticisms in silence: only from the young can one accept criticism, because only they see life as it really is. I would tell him everything, even those shadowy things which I did not reveal to those who knew me best, and he would advise me. It was he who warned me about Edward Shelley: 'He blows up easy and down again ditto,' he told me one evening. 'Don't mash him, Oscar.' His prescience was quite extraordinary. Who would have thought that a boy of humble origin would have shown more insight than I myself possessed? And that he would in the end demonstrate to me more loyalty and affection than the members of my own class? Perhaps it is not surprising, for when the real history of the world comes to be written it will reveal a great secret – that love and intelligence belong only to those who have been wounded by life.

I have said that with Robbie, and those whom I met with him, my friendship was social only. Although I sought for physical joy, I could not do so in their company. Sin should be solitary, and my expeditions were always alone. There were certain evenings when that fatal passion took possession of me – I would make an excuse to Constance, usually of an absurd kind, and then I would seek the night. I have never understood the nature of that fierce need which drove me forward: a scarlet speck fell across my brain, and all I could see were as yet unknown figures beckoning to me.

The curious thing is that I was perpetually disappointed and yet perpetually hopeful also – the expectations ran forward from the experience, as familiar and ever-renewed as the beak of the vulture became for Prometheus.

The mind has its Whitechapel as well as its West End, and, in my hunger for new sights of degradation and new sins, I loved to enter narrow rookeries. I wandered through the grey and sordid streets of the city with only my lust for company. I was warned by my companions that there were terrible dangers, as well as terrible delights, to be found there and that I was risking my life upon such expeditions. But what a fine thing, I would say, to risk one's entire life for a moment's pleasure. And in reality I was never afraid – doubtless that was the reason why I was never attacked. In pursuit of a certain house, or a certain alley, I would cross grassless squares where children slept in heaps upon the ground. I have seen mad women who in their poverty and neglect bayed to the moon to bring them release, the drunken fights which end in death in mean streets and the shadows which move quickly as the naptha lamps flicker. I saw all this, and I exulted in it. The sinners were sordid; the sins splendid.

In these first months, I went occasionally to a boys' brothel in the Lower Cut. It was disguised as a tailor's shop, although no clothes were ever made there. It often seemed curious to me that such a place should exist so close to the Strand – that such infamy and vice should burn so near to the fashionable world and yet not set it on fire. It was a narrow, tall building where on each floor a number of cheap wooden frames had been constructed to form a series of small rooms – each with its own squalid bed. I would be taken to one, and there a boy would come to me. The conversation was always the same – 'Got the dibs, guv'nor?' was a favourite phrase, I remember – and the lust was always the same, that wonderful liberation of the personality in a small, damp room. There, for the first time in my life, I felt wholly free. Sometimes, afterwards, the boys would talk to me – I was fascinated by their lives, and by the quite frank manner in which they talked of them. They were not ashamed of what they did: indeed, they considered themselves lucky for the opportunities of income which were now available to them.

But when I returned to Tite Street, and to my sleeping children, I felt shame – shame that I had allowed passion so to master my personality that I quite forgot my family and my own position as an artist. But shame is a curious thing: it is quite helpless in the face of more powerful emotions. I could not stop: I wanted the best, and I sought the worst. Like the philosopher Sardanapalus, I would have given a large sum of money to anyone who invented a new pleasure. In my madness I wished to sin beautifully, to perfect its techniques. The great mystery of Faust lies not in the separation between the intellect and the senses, but rather that sensation was for him an actual refinement of the intelligence. And so, in homage to German thought, I did not check my impulses – perhaps it would have been wrong to do so, for they would have turned to poison if they had been denied entrance into the world. I believe that the wildest profligate has, for that reason, a saner and better philosophy of life than the Puritan has. The Puritans are the great enemies of civilisation because they do not understand that it is founded upon joy.

You can understand, can you not, why I became as well known among a certain proportion of the lower classes as I was among those who ruled them? The narrow lanes off Oxford Street were quite familiar to me, and the boys of Piccadilly would whistle and hoot when by chance I passed them: it was for that reason, of course, that I rarely accompanied my wife to Swan and Edgar.

But, as I grew skilled in the ways of vice, I found other places in which to sate it. The names of those streets are burned in my imagination, as if I had entered the portals of Hell and seen the terrible words which Virgil points to: Blue Anchor Lane, Bombay Street, Grace's Alley, Wellclose Square. I searched the night-houses and the shameful corners of those streets for Lazarus, and when I found him I insisted upon kissing his lips: so I became ill of a great fever. There were houses where boys were auctioned to the old and to the depraved, rooms where strange lusts were gratified and new ones born. In the delirium of my lust, in such rooms I would kiss the boys all over their bodies; I could glimpse dimly then the secret of those sexual rites in which gods and spirits are raised.

Sometimes I would run from such places in fear and trembling; the least cry or shout would then seem to be raised against me, the prowling hansom with its amber light was like the carriage which would hurry me to Hell. If a policeman, on his rounds, shone his torch upon me as I hastened through the blackened, empty streets, I would start back in terror. The dirty yellow and blue light from the gas lamps would pursue me as I walked on, my heart beating in a hollow place. Such had my life become.

But there were times when I walked away from the night-houses with a sweet feeling of calm and well-being. It was in those moments of supreme physical release that wonderful lines and phrases would come to me unbidden; I would write them into my notebook and then use them in my art. I can recall composing an entire poem – 'Symphony in Yellow', it was called, in the days when my poems had names – as I walked home through the quiet streets of London in the early dawn. Those dawns were marvellous to me then; the darkness of the houses and the squares turned to the pearl grey shadows acquiring shape. As I walked by the Park, the waggons would pass me on their way to Covent Garden, and the countrymen would shout good morning to me. A city is like a human body: it can rise undefiled each day, and take on the raiments of wonder and of glory.

And in the same manner my own personality rose up. It was then that I experienced the strange fantasies of the double life. I sympathised truly with the poor and, through some atavistic instinct, wished to immerse myself in their lives. But it became an intellectual excitement to do so – to walk in the shadows of London and watch from a distance the brightness of a life that had been mine only hours before, and would be mine again as soon as I wished for it.

Sex came, in the end, to gratify my pride rather than my pleasure. I was head and not body, like the pictures of the goddess Laverna, for the memory of my sins was more pleasurable than the doing of them. They lent to me a quickened sense of joy, which sprang from my intellect and not my senses. I experienced every pleasure because I gave myself to none, but held myself apart, individual and indissoluble. I could see my own image in the eyes of those boys as I bent over them: I was two personalities – the one watching with heavy-lidded eyes the other's experience of bliss.

18 September 1900

I received this morning a letter from the Sphinx.

> My dear Oscar,
> I have written to you now on three occasions, but you have not
> been 'at home'. Pray tell me why. I hear nothing but gossip
> about you, which in the past I always assumed to be true – but
> only when it came from *you*. Without the god, the Sphinx is
> silent and can only scatter absurd messages on the parched
> land. Do write. Ever yours, dear Oscar –
> > Ada

I have drafted a letter in reply.

> My dear Sphinx,
> Your words strike me like thunder. Alas I have been living
> wisely but not well and have had, as a consequence, nothing
> whatever to write about. Do you remember that I once told you
> how terrible it was for a man to discover, at the end of his life,
> that he had always spoken nothing but the truth? Well, it is
> terrible to discover also that whatever one wrote turned to
> falsehood – and so now words frighten me. Dear Sphinx, I shall
> tell you a secret which, like all secrets, I expect you to forget. I
> have been writing the story of my life. You know, as I do, that
> the world does not care for memoirs from those it has already
> forgotten. And so I write for myself – at least I am a good
> audience. Do you remember how I would come to you amazed
> after my first nights, and ask you to explain to me in simple
> words what I had done? It was you who comforted me in my
> success, and understood me in my –

And then I threw away the letter; confessions on hotel notepaper
are always dreary. I have begun another:

My Dear Sphinx,

I was so charmed with hearing from you this morning that I must write a line and tell you how sweet and good it is of you to write to me. Robbie tells me that you are still making mortals immortal in *Punch*. I wish that you were writing for a Paris newspaper, that I could seek your work making the French tongue lovely.

I have been in great distress, but friends are kind to me and sometimes send me strange green notes which I use in restaurants. I long to dine with you again. Ever yours,

Oscar

That is all there is to be said, is it not?

19 September 1900

I have become a problem in modern ethics, as Symonds would say, although it seemed to me at the time that I was the solution. Everyone is talking about my particular disposition now for, as usual, I chose the proper dramatic moment to reveal my sexual infamy to the world. Even the Germans have become interested in the subject and, of all the extraordinary things that have happened to me, the most extraordinary may be that I shall be remembered not as an artist but as a case history, a psychological study to be placed beside Onan and Herodias. I might even be mentioned by Edward Carpenter in one of his more suggestive passages. I perfectly understand Carpenter, although he does not seem to understand himself – the consciousness of sin, he has written somewhere, displays a weakness in man. But our real weakness is far more interesting than that: we call activities sinful in order that we may enjoy them all the more fiercely.

The problem, as always in modern thought, is one of nomenclature. I am not inverted: I was diverted. If I am a Uranian, I spring from that part of the sky where Uranus is touched with the glory of the stars. For I hold male love to be of the highest kind, honoured by the philosophers who have considered it to be the type of ideal love, and by artists who have seen in the male figure the lineaments of spiritual beauty. Modern medicine, like an owl at noon which hoots blindly, so dazzled is it by the light, has invented new terms – but 'healthy' and 'diseased' are quite unsatisfactory as mental categories. Who would not rather be diseased as Leonardo and Winckelmann were, than healthy with Hall Caine and Mrs Cashel Hoey?

Every great creation involves a rupture of equilibrium, and the finest things in art have come from that fever of the passions which I and others like me have experienced. It was male love which inspired Michaelangelo in his perfect sonnets; it inspired Shakespeare to immortalise a young man in words of fire just as it guided the hands of Plato and of Marlowe.

When I became a servant of this love, I saw in it both the perfection and the fatality of the complete life. It held for me the innocence of all aspirations towards the beautiful, as well as the bitterness and weariness of self-knowledge. Caravaggio was moved by that love when he painted John the Baptist, with his delightfully child-like smile, and his eyes which have already seen the horror of things to come. In that image are both seduction and despair, innocent need and troubled satiety.

Bobbie is interested in Socratic works of a rather different kind, however. He would take me to a small bookshop in St James's Street which had, I believe, a French name – it was a sort of circulating library, although the circulation was of a limited and select kind. There was one work, *Teleny*, which passed from hand to hand and to which I added small touches of my own. It was a story of corrupt and dangerous passions, although much of it read like *Gray's Anatomy*. Rabelaisian literature has never been of particular interest to me – it is always deficient in form, and stumbles under the weight of too much content – and *Teleny* provided only the crudest materials for an artistic fiction. But I did not mock the book: I was pleased to read deeply in all aspects of homoerotic literature, in the records of dead love as much as in the celebration of living ones. For, even when I was caught in my sins, I was convinced of the essential virtue of Greek love: men can live in perfect equality, each finding in the other the image of his own soul. Men and women can never live in peace – they either destroy each other, or bore each other, which is worse. When in the *Symposium* Socrates quite refutes the arguments of Aristophanes – that man and woman are but two torn natures striving to be reunited – he proclaimed a great truth which modern civilisation, with the possible exception of Ibsen, seems to have forgotten: men and women are not complementary, they are antagonistic. The great romances have always been between men.

But such love depends upon true equality and, in my madness, I used the spirit of Socrates to bless unholy unions. Instead of seeking a companion, I went into the gutter and saw my own image outlined in the dust only. I went to the young because the young have no conscience – that was why I loved them.

There is a story in Celtic literature of Tirnan-Og, the country of the young. Neither age nor death is to be found there; neither tears nor hollow laughter hold dominion. The bard Oisen, desiring to learn the secrets of that place, travelled there under cover of darkness. He found the enchanted country and dwelt there for three hundred years. But he grew heart-sick for his previous life, and for the country of his birth, and returned by the way he had come. The moment his feet touched his native earth, his three hundred years fell upon him. His figure was bent double, and all the cares which troubled the world during those long years fell upon him also. Simple stories have simple morals. One should never pursue the young: in doing so, one loses one's own youth.

I, too, had grown weary of my wanderings through London: I did not wish to abandon my pleasures, only to find them closer to home. And so where my sins had once been solitary, now I found a companion who could guide me. Alfred Taylor, whom I met at the Crown, had like me a weakness for boys – and men of our kind seek each other out for our weaknesses and not for our strengths. He promised me adventures: he pandered to my instincts and brought me those companions whom I sought. Taylor was to be tried with me at the Old Bailey; he was offered immunity from prosecution if he would testify against me, but he refused. From such moments in life are saints born. One noble act, like that of Mary Magdalene, can obliterate with perfumes all the sins of the world: although I believe Alfred's hair was rather longer than the Magdalene's.

I liked Taylor because he was improbable. He had invented for himself, in his rooms near Westminster, a world of gaiety and of pleasure, of strange scents and cloths. He understood that although reality cannot be imagined – it is too awful for that – it can be made imaginary. And so I would take a cab to his lodgings, to meet his 'pullets' as he charmingly described them; sometimes he would bring them to me in the private rooms of restaurants. There the champagne flowed freely and, after the champagne, the love.

They were not bad boys. I know that some of them testified against me when I stood in the dock, but I understand that. Some had been frightened by threats, and others had been lured by the prospect of gold. I never judge those who amuse me and, in truth, the curious lives of these boys interested me. It seemed that they were walking along the same perilous wire as myself – although my fall was to be greater. Many of them came from a family, or a background, where a commonplace life would have made it easy for them to be virtuous; but they had the courage to experience

114

more dangerous sensations. I listened to their stories for hours, and in recompense I gave them presents, small gifts only, although at my trials they were handed around to the jury as if they were relics from some barbaric faith. When Alfred Taylor and I found ourselves alone, we too would talk continually of our own adventures: they were fascinating, terribly fascinating, to me.

Sometimes in Taylor's lodgings there were parties of an intimate kind. Alfred had a particular interest in women's clothes and, since I have been from my aesthetic period an expert on the subject, I would assist him in the choice of hats and gowns which he would wear to entertain the company. Some of the young men took a similarly advanced view on the question of modern dress, and with Alfred they would perform masques and dramas which often descended to a Biblical level. On one occasion, Alfred and two boys performed *Salomé* in my honour – it was that scarlet drama's first and only performance in England, and I was delighted by the spirit it inspired in them. Charlie Mason, who had quite recovered from his arrest in Cleveland Street, played Salomé with the gestures of the divine Sarah herself and Alfred was a magnificent, if somewhat too feminine, Herodias. It was a delightful evening and, at the close, the boys crowned me with lilies – there are no garlands of myrtle to be found in England – and carried me around the room. I made a little speech, in which I congratulated them for their quite unaffected performances.

I cannot myself act, unless I am delivering my own lines, but I was once persuaded by Alfred to assist at one of his performances. My fondness for the Queen is well known – I am surprised she has not written to me lately, but I am told that she is busy organising the South African campaign. Indeed, Alfred was continually telling me of my remarkable resemblance to her: in what particular aspect I, of course, cannot say. And so on one evening, at a new year's celebration – it must have been 1894, one year before my fall – I was draped in black and a small but delightful crown was placed upon my head. I admit that the role suited me perfectly, and I spoke quietly but humbly about my service to the nation and to dear, departed Albert. Then they all rose and sang God Save The Queen – I was much affected, and promised them the 'Queen's touch' on Maundy Thursday. I do not think I was ever quite the same again.

Do you understand now why I enjoyed the company of these boys? With them my years left me; I did not feel the weight of a reputation which was even then threatening to crush me. I enjoyed reading to them from my plays and the boys' laughter – or, sometimes, their sombre concern at a particularly humorous turn in the drama – was for me enchanting. Alfred and I would take each character in turn – I remember that I was an emphatic Mrs Erlynne – and there were occasions when I would improvise in dialogue and impress even myself with the result. The boys admired me and, like Jesus, I have always performed my better miracles for those who have believed.

I like to be seen with the boys – some of my friends thought it scandalous that I should do so, but the greater scandal is to be ashamed of one's companions. I was never that: I loved to walk with them through the crowded thoroughfares of London, or to visit with them the public places of entertainment. I remember once going with Charlie Lloyd to the Crystal Palace. I had visited it previously in order to lecture there – it was a place of grim memories.

It was full of the smell of fresh buns and fresh paint, the shrieks from the monkey house blending quite successfully with the cries of the children as they watched with fascination the head of a pantomime clown, some twelve feet across, on which the eyes and mouth opened with the aid of a mechanism. Even the parents seemed impressed: it struck me as curious that the machinery could be such a source of wonder, but no doubt there will be a future for it in museums and circuses when it has vanished from our industries. There was also a Handel Festival during our visit, which Charlie quite rightly declined to attend, and we turned our attention instead to the toy-stalls in which glass waterfalls trickled in landscapes of Virginian cork and Swiss peasants valsed: all for a penny. The nineteenth century is an extraordinary thing, although only in its trivial aspects.

Charlie Lloyd had no conversation. 'Jolly good, Oscar' was, I believe, his only phrase. I would torment him with questions, about Bimettalism or the Irish question, and he would simply smile at me. He had a pale, unlined face – an advantage I ascribe entirely to his diet. He seemed to live entirely off potted meats, Palmers biscuits and Bovril. He was almost an advertisement. I could not tempt him to restaurants, and I did not wish to tempt him to bed. But he interested me: he was a perfect type. I possessed a gold cross which in a moment of enthusiasm I had given to my first great love in Dublin, Florence Balcombe. Of course I retrieved it immediately on her marriage, to an actor. While we were at the Crystal Palace, I gave it to Charlie – it pleased me that it should change hands in so obvious a fashion. I do not know what he did with it: perhaps he ate it.

In those days the theatre was always the main attraction – not the serious theatre where the middle classes learn of the difficulties of their lives, but the music halls. With Sidney Mavor and Fred Atkins I would go to the Tivoli or the Empire, to see the ventriloquists, funambulists and Ethiopian comedians. Sidney's favourite was always Mr Stratton, known popularly as Dan Leno – that droll creature who adopts the accents and attitudes of the lower classes with a humour that is both perceptive and benign. There was something quite alarming in the manner with which he was able to mimic the voice of a washer-woman or the strange gait of a variety actress: it was as if the glory and the darkness of the London streets had enshrined themselves in this little personage, leaving him visibly bowed and drained.

I sent round my card to him at the end of one performance, and he welcomed me with such graciousness and affability that I was charmed at once. 'Mr Wilde,' he said to me in that deep voice which was quite unlike his stage manner, 'I am a comedian and you are a dramatist, but we both have our patter, don't we?' I agreed – how could I not? 'The secret, in my reckoning, is to bring them close to crying and then boost them up again. That's the ticket.' I smiled, and said nothing.

One theatrical incident I shall never be able to forget: it was at the Trocadero, before it became a restaurant, although some people profess not to know the difference. Arthur Faber, who was in those days a well-known impersonator, came upon the stage. After a few rather conventional scenes, involving drunks, policemen and the usual melodrama of real life, he picked up a cane with a gold top, placed around his shoulders a large fur coat, arranged his body into a grotesquely bloated shape, and sang some bawdy lyric.

It was with sudden horror that I realised he was impersonating me. It was done with much humour, but it was as if I had been slapped across the face. I saw myself at that instant as others saw me, and I felt a terrible sense of fatality – as though this creature on the stage was too preposterous to survive; the hoots and calls from the pit were the cries of those baying for blood. I did not understand why this should be so, and I left the theatre hurriedly.

117

20 September 1900

Now that, like Dante, I have walked into the twilight world, the ghosts of the past come hurrying to greet me. There were other boys, whose names did not emerge at the time of my trials; and, although I was convicted of many sins I did not commit, there were others which were not placed in the indictment against me. When young men wrote to me about my work, I would arrange interviews with them and plan schemes of seduction. I needed continually the excitement of the chase, and did not care about the nature of the quarry. So it was that I ended in the hands of the lowest renters, like Wood and Taylor. I liked them because they were dangerous – simply that.

But, although I longed for the pleasures which they and their kind provided, I did not enjoy them when they had been found. My physical excitation waned and, although I used to fondle the boys, it was no more than helpless affection – not the sordid and mechanical delirium which has been trumpeted to the world. My real joy was to watch two boys together in the various acts of love, and to pleasure myself as they did so. I think I have been primarily a spectator always – I had become a spectator even of my own life, so that everything seemed to come to me from an infinite distance. And I enjoyed the spectacle of love, I admit it – it is a strange illusion that only in one's member is lust to be found. That is a modern heresy. The pleasures of watching seemed greater to me, for there is also a lust of the mind.

But you can understand, can you not, why I experienced a sense of damnation in the midst of this life, and why I was drinking so excessively that even my friends began to whisper about me? When intelligence peeped through these pleasures, I became horrified at my delirium and, in my despair, threw myself back into it again. I trembled when I read Anatole France's scarlet tragedy, *Thaïs*, of the despair that succeeds excess, the torment that follows the swift feet of riot.

But indeed I think in the midst of my lust I longed for an end to it – that might be the secret of my fall. I was weary of all that I knew, and I grew terribly tired. I could not now look upon Constance or my young sons without shame. I had allowed my real work to fall away from me. In the last years I wrote only for money, the money which I spent on company unworthy of me, and the applause, the applause which turned too quickly to the hoots and catcalls of derision. I had lost myself in my sins; with my own hands I had blinded myself and I stumbled into the pit. I can write no more: I must lie down and rest my head.

21 September 1900

When I first entered my 'new life', three years after my marriage,
I was so immersed in my sins that I did no work of a serious kind.
But the strange ritual of my fate was already turning unholy things
into sacraments, and I had begun to see artistic possibilities in the
double life. As it was for Janus, who looked both backwards and
forwards, so it was for me: I could see the world more completely.
And, if I became possessed by my sins, it was with the fever that
allows one to speak freely for the first time.

My first work was primarily of a critical nature. The dialogues in
which I outlined my philosophy sprang fully armed from my
conversations with Robert Ross in Tite Street: conceived in
laughter, they had that joy within them which pierces all
mysteries. I formed a philosophy out of Egotism and out of the
self-consciousness of Art which, like that of Rousseau, was 'de nier
ce qui est, et d'expliquer ce qui n'est pas'.

Under the guise of paradox, I exposed the illusions of my period
and set forth a larger and saner reality in their place. I do not agree
with everything which I wrote then, but that is the price of perfect
expression – it ceases to belong to oneself, and belongs instead to
the world.

In all my first writings, from the portrait in chiaroscuro of
Thomas Wainewright, the poisoner, to the relatively straight-
forward manner of my *Soul of Man under Socialism*, I wished to
express a philosophy which was complete in itself because I, too,
would then be complete: I fashioned a style which perfectly
expressed my attitudes and at the same time gilded my experience with shining words. It is true that I was writing about the
charms of indolence and the pleasures of the artist at a time when
my health and nerves were seriously affected by the life I was then
leading. But mine was the dream of the alchemist: the transforma-
tion of the weary heart into the unwearied spirit. The nineteenth

century is a sensuous, sordid age, but I wished to subtilise the senses, to arrange them in an order higher than that which the commercial classes aspired to. I thought I could mingle in the sensuous world without shame or loss, and come back from it with fresh perceptions – just as in my imagination I could enter the house of the poor and return with a philosophy which quite understood the nature of poverty. And that angered my contemporaries. They did not wish to see their sins in any light – not even one which refined them, and made them the elements of a new spirituality in which the fine instinct for beauty was the dominant characteristic.

But one's philosophy is always less interesting than oneself and I believe that throughout my writing, even that which is concerned with beautiful, timeless things, I wished to reveal myself to the world as a man marked by fresh sensations. In *The Portrait of Mr W.H.*, that extraordinary essay in which I reveal the identity of the boy who haunts Shakespeare's sonnets, I limned a portrait of perfect masculine beauty, in which both sexes have left their touch. This book was my homage to Greek love, and never had I put my learning to more artful use. It was of no concern to me if the facts were accurate or inaccurate: I had discerned a truth which was larger than that of biography and history, a truth not merely about Shakespeare but about the nature of all creative art. And, even though I invented the name of the boy actor, Willie Hughes, at whose shrine Shakespeare had brought such a wonderful offering, I will be quite astounded if Willie Hughes did not exist: at any moment I expect him to be discovered by an Oxford scholar. Nature always follows Art.

But that book was simply an entertainment. My first really impressive work was *The Picture of Dorian Gray*. It was not a début but it was the next best thing, a scandal. It could not have been otherwise: I wanted to rub the faces of my generation in their own century, at the same time as I wished to create a novel which would defy the canons of conventional English fiction. It might have been written in French, for it seems to me that its charm lies in the fact that it is quite without meaning of any kind, just as it is without any fashionable moral. It is an odd book, filled with the vivacity and the strange joy with which it was written. I fashioned it quickly and without serious preparation and, as a result, the whole of my personality dwells somewhere within it: but I do not think I know where. I exist in every character, although I cannot pretend to comprehend the forces which impel them forward. All I fully realised, as I wrote it, was the necessity that it should end in disaster: I could not reveal such a world without watching it collapse in shame and weariness.

I was at first surprised by the hostile reaction which *Dorian Gray* provoked, and it was only when I had finished these first works that I realised what I had done: I had effectively challenged conventional society on every possible front. I had mocked its artistic pretensions, and derided its social morality; I had shown the hovels of the poor as well as the houses of the depraved, but I had also shown that in its own homes there lurked hypocrisy and conceit. I date my downfall from that period – it was the moment when the prison gates swung open for me, and awaited my arrival.

But the irony is that I held out my own hands to be tied. For an artist is not a savant: the difference between his work and that of a philosopher, or even a journalist, is that his own personality enters and defines his work. Although I was revealing the sins of the world, I was also disclosing the sins which I harboured; the vanity and hypocrisy were mine, just as the vice was mine, and the fierce joy of denunciation was mine also.

Of course my wife knew nothing of this and, as a result, I could not be near her when she read my work; she said nothing to me which could not be construed as loyal admiration, but she was troubled – I saw that. It was only when I wrote about marriage that she became visibly hurt. She told me that she had wept when she read some of the things I had written on that subject – it was something to do with the 'life of deception' that a perfect marriage entails – but in my infatuation with my own genius I hardly understood what she meant. She much preferred my stories in *The House of Pomegranates* which, in expurgated form, she would read to the children. I believe she even managed to extract a moral from them: where I had seen only the horror and the impermanence of the world, she found love and beauty. It was like her to do so.

Those stories were largely unremarked by the public, however. Now that my name was attached to infamous work, they wanted only to be amused or shocked. And I was infinitely obliging: immediately after I had completed my first comedy, *Lady Windermere's Fan*, I set to work on *Salomé*. Although they are written in different styles – *Salomé* had to be composed in French as well, since my serious characters always think in that language –

they are not so different in feeling. I have always wished an audience to understand them in the same way – they are both gilded creations where, instead of the masks of classical drama, my actors are shielded by perfect sentences. That is all.

It was only in my drama that I saw both the horror and comedy of life, the brilliant success and the grotesque passion. When I was being applauded for the wit of *Lady Windermere's Fan*, it was quite natural that in *Salomé* I should create a play in which the dominant moods were mystery and terror. I wanted my entire personality to be revealed, so that I could gain the plaudits of the world equally for that which was inchoate and dark within me as for that which was smart or amusing. I believe that if *Salomé* had not been banned by the Lord Chamberlain, and had been performed on the London stage, my subsequent life would have changed utterly. I would have presented myself so fully to the world that I would not have wished to continue my double life of sin and shame. But, as long as I was known as the author only of witty comedies, I felt incomplete and sought for expression elsewhere.

And my comic plays are connected, I see that now, by the consciousness of sin which is struggling to come into the light – sin as doleful as that of Phèdre, as laughable as that of Falstaff. I turned it into melodrama, and of course rendered it more serious by doing so; I thought of it as an artistic device and forgot that, as an artist, I would not therefore be able to free myself from it. In *A Woman of No Importance* I played with a theme which intrigued and frightened me both at once: that of a relationship between a younger and an older man. The boy is dazzled by the cultivation of the man, the man by the beauty of the boy. I have the situation by heart, you might say.

But *An Ideal Husband* was the play which most closely resembled the terrible drama of my life – the husband's fear is that of scandal. A letter arrives to expose him: just such a letter came to my house, brought by two blackmailers of the lowest kind. But in that play I made it clear that I do not give in to threats. I wrote the passages of denunciation and pride with all the passion of a man convinced of the truth of his own narrative. Of course I resolved all the problems in the final scene, just as I expected to do in my own life. I believed that I was a great enough dramatist to turn life itself into a drama.

So it was that in my final comedy, *The Importance of Being Earnest*, I mocked life even at the time when it was showing me its most terrible aspects, when I was pursued by blackmailers no less assiduously than by the mad, pantomimic dance of Queensberry. I wrote the play in great agony of mind, when I knew that disaster and humiliation were about to fall on me. But it seems to me now that by the strange alchemy of the artistic life it was the threat of ruin which wounded me into life. I have always asserted that out of joy only can creative work spring, but it is possible that out of fear and pain, also, joyous words can come. In the chronicle of Limburg, there is a story about the lovely *aubades* of the fourteenth century which the young men and women of Germany then sang. The chronicle tells us that the author of these lyrics was a clerk afflicted with leprosy, living apart from the world. He went through the streets with an enormous rattle, giving notice of his approach. And the people shrank from his affliction, even as they knew he was the maker of their songs. I have proved that to be a true story, have I not?

And so I played with life until the end, even though I knew that life was also playing with me. We understood each other completely and, when life and imagination are so much in harmony, only comedy can properly express it. I constructed fine, light work, as sensuous as Maeterlinck, as witty as Sheridan. And yet I carved, also, a pillory for myself in which I would be placed for eternity. Look, people will say, this is the kind of heartless and absurd drama which leads to a prison cell.

23 September 1900

A postcard has come from Bosie: it is strange that so modern a poet should wish to write in so open a fashion. It reads: 'I am coming to Paris with Tom next week. I expect that you will require dinner.' He has signed it, absurdly, 'Lord Alfred Douglas'. Really, it leaves very little to the imagination, except for the sudden appearance of a third party: who is Tom? What is he? But then Bosie has always believed that life should run ahead of the imagination, and if possible exhaust it, whereas I have always helped the imagination to outstrip life. That was why we affected each other so fatally: I disproved all of his theories and he could never understand mine.

Lionel Johnson, the ochre-coloured poet, brought him to see me in Tite Street. Bosie had read *The Picture of Dorian Gray* in, I regret to say, a magazine, and had determined to meet its author. No book has had such fatal consequences for me. He told me later that he felt he had read in *Dorian Gray* the secret history of his own life: I was the magus who had provided the words to unlock the mystery of his soul. He was absurdly romantic, of course, but that was his charm. And, when I first saw him, I was dazzled. He had what Pater calls the pagan melancholy of beautiful youth, who sees all the corruption of the world and is yet unstained by it.

I was lost as soon as I loved him, because I had transgressed the one commandment which modern society has bound in hoops of brass. When Christ said, 'Your sins will be forgiven you because you have loved,' the English public says, 'Your crimes will be punished because you have dared to love.' My affection for Lord Alfred Douglas gave a beauty and a dignity to the love between men which the English could not look upon without horror: that is why they sent me to prison. I could have had all the renters I wanted; the boys who sell themselves in Southwark or Clerkenwell are of no account, and it was only to be expected that I would

125

shower red gold upon them in exchange for their pale bodies. That, after all, is the theory of capitalism. But that I should have conceived of a higher love, a love between equals – that they could not accept, and for that there would be no forgiveness. Although that love has been celebrated by Shakespeare, by Hafiz and by Virgil in his second eclogue, it is a love that dare not speak its name because it is nameless – like the secret word for God in Indian mythology, to utter it is to be rendered accursed.

Even when I first knew Bosie, there was a sense of damnation about him, like the perfumed flowers which flourish only in marshland. It was that sense of damnation which drew us together just as, finally, it tore us apart. It made us grow more reckless in our love, but with a recklessness that finally destroyed me. I, who thought I could mock the world in my essays and epigrams, found my sticking point.

Bosie wrote to me, some six months after we had met, begging for my help in a strange affair. He had conceived a passion for a quite young boy. The parents, it seemed, had not objected to this passion – indeed they actively encouraged it, and even invited Bosie into their own house so that it might continue in a less than platonic manner. And then the simple thing happened, as the simple thing always does: they blackmailed him, and threatened to expose him to his parents. It would have been a hideous scandal since the boy was quite the wrong age for such adventures. And so Bosie wrote to me for assistance, pleading that he had 'sinned only as Dorian Gray sinned'. It was naïve of him, but then he has always possessed a certain innocence: for innocence is the strongest of virtues, and can exist in the midst of an intensely dissipated life.

Naturally, I helped him. I visited Edwin Levy, a 'private agent' whose name never appears in the newspapers, a Jew who knows everyone's business and is therefore in a position to protect his clients admirably. Through him, a proposition was put to the parents of the boy. They accepted, and the affair was silenced. I had only to endure a lecture from Levy, warning me of my association with those who courted danger in so assiduous a fashion as 'the young Lord'. He knew, or suspected, that I was living in a similar manner, which is why he advised total discretion in all my affairs. 'This young man,' I recall him saying, 'is dangerous for you.' But it was precisely that which attracted me to him – I loved Bosie as one would love a wounded animal.

When I was in prison I wrote Bosie a long and terrible letter, in which the affair at Oxford was only the beginning of a chronicle of woe. Bosie never mentions it now, which is wise and just of him – more just than I deserve. It was a terrible letter because I placed on him that burden of guilt which belonged on my shoulders only and, in my spite and bitterness, I lent to it a weight which Atlas himself could not endure without groaning. I appeared in that letter as a victim, an innocent out of a melodrama who walks unsuspecting into the dark forest where giants part the leaves and peer at him. But it was not so. I said in that letter that it was necessary for me to look upon the past with different eyes. Well, now I must try to do so.

Much has been written about the love of an older man for a younger man, but very little has been said about the passion which the younger man can conceive for the older. That love is far more dangerous for it breeds pride in him who is loved. I became Bosie's idol rather than his companion. He fed my vanity with his attentions, just as I took his character and moulded it into my own image. As a result, we became inseparable. I stayed with him at Oxford and, when we grew bored with the country, we would take rooms at the Albemarle or the Savoy.

Whatever extravagances he may have possessed, I nurtured; whatever base instincts he had, I encouraged; whatever experiences he wished to taste, I provided for him. The course of our life in London is now public knowledge, I believe. I took him into the really fashionable world, which was his by right, and then into the darker world of the streets, which became his by choice. I instilled in him a love of the exotic, in food and drink no less than in more unfamiliar pleasures. We would dine at the Savoy and have supper at Willis's; after that, I would lead him into the Inferno.

As we became more frenzied in our pursuit of pleasure, London itself became an unreal city, a play of brilliant lights and crowds and mad laughter. My boldness infected Bosie for, in order to show his love, he imitated me to the point where he would, in my place, do the things I had only dreamed of – and things I dared not dream of. He wished to become precisely the portrait of him which I had formed in my imagination and so he became terrible, because my imagination was terrible also.

I did not reckon then the cost, to him and to others. I would invite him to dine in Tite Street with Constance and myself, and I forced him to play a vicious double game. We would talk politely and seriously and then, perhaps after an unfortunate remark by Constance, Bosie would burst out in mad laughter and I would laugh also. My wife did not understand, of course, and retreated into bewildered silence. She did not know the truth then, but there were times when she must have suspected it although she said nothing. She would take Vyvyan and Cyril into the country, and in the house which should have been sacred to me because it had harboured my children I encouraged Bosie to slake his perversities.

In my trial I was accused of taking boys back with me to the Savoy. It is true, but I took them there for Bosie's sake. I did not care to indulge in those sins which he, with the violent passion of youth, enjoyed so freely. I have explained how great for me was the joy in watching others' pleasure, and it became my habit to watch Bosie and his companions in the acts of love. Bosie sometimes would look up and smile at me – it was a wonderful, cruel smile which I myself had painted upon his face.

My mother would write to me of Constance's feelings, of her loneliness and unhappiness, and I would write to Bosie about mine. I would gild our sins with phrases and persuade him that in excess is to be found a terrible purity, the purity of the gods. I told him to seek the 'liberty of the heart', although there was no such liberty to be found.

I did no work of an artistic kind: I found the lover's crown of myrtle more satisfying than the poet's crown of bays. I had thought that, since love is the root of all wonder, it must also be the source of great creation. Now I realise that love is merely a substitute for such work. It creates the conditions, but prevents one from employing them. It provokes the mood, but stifles the desire to express it. And indeed at this time, some two years before my disgrace, I was tired of my art. Although others were prophesying for me a marvellous future as a dramatist, I think I knew even then that my work was coming to an end.

The more fiercely I loved Bosie, the more bitterly I accused myself for allowing my life to come to such a point; and then, by the strange alchemy of passion, I grew to accusing him also. At one moment I would spur him on to fresh excesses simply, in my delirium, to see to what lengths he would go in order to please me. And than at another I would grow frightened of him. I believe that the gods themselves are frightened of the world which they have fashioned, and I became afraid of what Bosie might say or do. When the mist of pleasure dropped from my eyes, I would counsel caution and he would laugh. I would suggest a temporary separation, and he would rage at me.

There were hideous scenes between us, both in London and in the country. Bosie's fury was demented – it was the fury of a creature caught in a trap which is not of its devising. He knew only too well what I had made of him, what scenery I had painted for him, and what lines I had given him to speak. But he had grown to love the worst part of himself, and that worst part was me.

I recall one occasion when we were lunching in the Berkeley Hotel. I told him that I had received a letter from his father, the Marquess of Queensberry.

'And what did the little man say? Did he say anything about me?'

'It was an entirely personal letter – he only spoke about himself. He says that he is being made a fool of, and that our conduct is humiliating him.'

'He's an oaf to think that anyone cares tuppence for him.'

'He also accuses me of practising unnatural vices. That is absurd of him: I never practise. I am perfect.'

'And what else?'

'He says I have corrupted you.'

Bosie grew angry: it was extraordinary how his features changed under the impress of passion.

'We must be more careful, Bosie.'

'You are a coward, Oscar. You look like a woman, and you have the manners of a woman.'

'But I think he means to watch for us.'

At that Bosie laughed, but it was a terrible laugh. To my horror, he produced a pistol from his pocket and waved it in the air.

'He's a dog!' he shouted. 'And I will shoot him like a dog if he comes near me.'

And then, to my astonishment, he fired at the chandelier in the middle of the dining room. It provoked the most dreadful scene, of course, and we were asked to leave the restaurant.

The event was paraded in the newspapers, and I believe the *Chronicle* suggested that it was I who had fired the shot. I was in great agony of mind, for I knew that something evil had come into my life.

In London we were pointed at in the streets. I pretended indifference – I am used to such attentions – and naturally Bosie imitated me. But he was hurt, deeply hurt, to become an object of derision among the common people and, in his arrogance, he decided to surpass even their conception of his infamy. It was, I believe, the bad blood of his race that spurred him forward – like Julien Sorel, the only thing that seemed real to him was his fear of ridicule.

And so we fled from our companions and our familiar haunts. We travelled to Algiers, and at peril to our lives visited low dens where wreaths of opium curled around the blackened roofs. We visited Florence, and by our behaviour scandalised even the Italians. It was here that I began my *Florentine Tragedy*. I fashioned a plot in which a wife spurs on her lover to kill her own husband: in passion, for me, only the doom remained, and the red mist of doom which hides men from each other's sight. We were lost, both of us lost.

When we returned to England, Bosie, like a guilty thing, turned upon his accusers. The strange pride of his race reasserted itself, and he vented his fierce scorn, no longer upon me who led him forward in the paths of vice, but upon his father, who now goaded him with threats and abuse. I became part of the war between Bosie and Queensberry but, like a glass, I simply magnified the rays of their mutual enmity – although I was the one to burn.

But Bosie never betrayed me: he stood by me during the trials and, after my imprisonment, never ceased to write letters on my behalf. But, alas, in my own letter from prison I betrayed him. I knew that it was within my power to show him an image of himself that was so cleverly conceived that he would accept it at once – just as he had once accepted Dorian Gray as his own picture. When I wrote in my ballad that one kills the thing one loves, I meant it precisely.

Of course I have gone back to him. It is part of the terrible symmetry of fate that I should need Bosie now when he no longer needs me. He scatters banknotes in my direction, although I believe he knows that he is giving alms to the man who destroyed him, and that he is kissing the lips of the man who betrayed him with his words. But I shall see him next week, and he will buy me dinner. No doubt I shall charm Tom, and he will grow jealous. It is curious how, when the most fiery passions have passed, there is left only a strange emptiness.

25 September 1900

Scandal has always followed my name, of course, but the rumours about me began in earnest during the controversy over *Dorian Gray* and *The Portrait of Mr W . H .*; at first they made me quite ill. I thought that I had created works of the imagination, and yet I was assailed on all sides by whispers of terrible perversities. I was nervous, with the nervousness of one who cannot calculate the effects which he is producing, and I could not sleep or rest. I thought that in Art I might conceal myself, and yet in the newspapers my books were taken as an extraordinary form of self-revelation. There would have been no use in reciting to the *St James Gazette* the first law of the imagination, that in his work the artist is someone other than himself – it would have come as too great a shock. And, in any event, I have always been used as a whipping boy by journalists.

But it was quite otherwise when my social life was affected. As a result of the scandal, I was blackballed from the Savile Club and insulted in the Hogarth. Henley snubbed me in the street on the day *Dorian Gray* was published in volume form and, to complete his extraordinary idea of manners among civilised people, he never ceased to attack me in his own newspaper –Henley of all people, whom I had invited to my house and who had proclaimed from the rooftops his devotion to art and the things of art. The man who could abuse me after that is capable of anything. Those who have kissed Apollo – even, like Henley, if it has only been on the cheek – should not lie down in the street with Thersites.

By the time I was writing comedies, my reputation was in alien hands, and I could no more have controlled it than I could have silenced the wind. Of course I became an even greater attraction at the more advanced dinner parties – people wished to lift the mask from my face and find the one which they themselves had placed there. I grew used to this. I became accustomed to the sudden silence when I entered the room and I did not object to it: I thought of it as the silence of an audience before the curtain rises. But Constance felt it, and grew ashamed.

But if Society talked about me behind my back, the lower classes had the courage to insult me to my face. I was as well known as the Bank of England, although I am in some respects more solid, and there were areas of Piccadilly and Leicester Square where I could not walk without provoking public attention. I remember once standing outside Fortnum and Mason while my wife was making some small purchases – I did not accompany her into the shop, for fear that I might recognise one or two of the assistants – when a young woman passed me, turned her head, looked me in the face and laughed, a strange, mad laugh which left me shaken and bereft of feeling. It was as if she had found my heart and placed a dagger there, for hers was the laughter of Atropos, who cuts the thread of life.

From the beginning, even when I first left my house in search of dangerous adventure, I feared that I should be found out – but that made the final reckoning all the more surprising to me. I had believed that such fear might act as an amulet, and prevent what was most feared from occurring. But it was not so: what was dreaded came to pass. And it is curious, is it not, that although I could face scandal in public, although I could mock it or turn it aside in conversation, I could not endure it alone? I would lie on my bed and, in a fever of imagination, conjure up scenes of doom and damnation which rivalled those of Dante or of Jeremiah, scenes in which I of course was the principal character and the world was a malevolent thing which harried me. I felt helpless: sometimes I would cry out in my sleep where, once, I had laughed.

When I began to be blackmailed, I lost my head. I was once found with a boy in the Albemarle Hotel, by one of the staff there. Although I paid the servant what was apparently a large sum for his silence, several times he came to my house and asked for 'Mr Wilde'. I would hand him a bank-note and demand that he leave: when my wife asked me who it was, I said only that it was a tradesman who had called with a bill. But there were others, many others; some of them, like Wood and Clibborn, would not let me rest and pursued me from Tite Street to the Café Royal. I felt like a wounded animal assailed on all sides, and I longed for oblivion, in the grave or any other place. I was to find that peace in prison.

But, although my fate was rushing towards me, I did not think that eventually it would take the form of the Marquess of Queensberry. To be strung up by a clown, and kicked by a pantomime horse: that was my destiny. Some people are terrible because they have no law of being and thrust themselves blindly into the world: Queensberry was such a one. He had no feelings save those of anger and revenge. He had the habit of 'speaking his mind' without realising that he had no mind to speak of. On the few occasions I met him, he said things which I did not understand. He was mad, and I have always felt a terrible unease in the presence of mad people. When he started his campaign against me and Bosie, I was frightened only because I knew there would be no constancy and no predictability to his course – and that such was his rage that no words of mine could avert it.

Queensberry would have put Christ on the cross again to see me ruined. He hounded me through London; he would warn the managers of hotels not to receive me, and he would send absurd communications to the restaurants where I was accustomed to dine, threatening to cause a 'scene' of hideous proportions. With the madness of his family, Bosie goaded him with telegrams or open postcards, outlining in wonderful detail our itinerary for the day, and then he would turn to me for praise for doing so. Queensberry even called at my house one evening – fortunately, Constance and the children were in Worthing – and spoke to me in the most insulting fashion. I threw him out, but the taint was there: the beast had penetrated the labyrinth. When I told Bosie he laughed: it simply gave him another opportunity for a telegram.

Not satisfied with destroying the harmony of my house, Queensberry attacked my professional life by appearing at the St James's Theatre with a bunch of vegetables. It was absurd: and, if I had been able to convince myself that it was only absurd, I might have become merely another spectator of the melodrama as it unfolded. But I lost my head, alas, and became a participant in it.

I was not the only object of his vengeance. The terrible scandal about Rosebery was fomented by him, a scandal which was to affect me more than I then had reason to suspect. Queensberry accused him of unnatural vices, and carried about everywhere with him a picture of Rosebery which was entitled 'the new Tiberius': it was quite obscene. But he was not content merely with innuendoes of a malicious kind. By chance, he discovered the proof he was seeking – although there is proof of guilt everywhere, for those who wish to find it.

He wrote to Rosebery about a certain supper party at Bourne End in which Queensberry's eldest son, Drumlanrig, was found to play a larger role, shall we say, than the private secretary as which Rosebery employed him. He threatened to reveal Rosebery's relationship with his son to the world. In his distress Drumlanrig, who imagined that he had betrayed his employer no less than his family, took his life with a gun. He was found in a field in Somerset. Of course the matter was at once 'hushed up', and only a few knew the truth of it, but it was a tragedy that cast a dark shadow over my own life simply because it promised no escape from the wrath of the scarlet Marquess except under the most lurid circumstances.

I met Rosebery a little after this. He avoided me, of course – he was a politician, and politicians mix with artists at their own risk – but I could see in his face the pain which he was suffering. He gave me his hand when we were introduced; he looked at me – only momentarily, but it was a look of fear – and then turned away.

On all sides I was urged to take stern and definite action against my persecutor. When Constance heard from our cook that he had visited the house – if her cooking is anything to go by, it would have been a melodramatic account – she was outraged and insisted that I took steps to prevent him doing so again. I went so far as to consult my solicitors, but at first I drew back from the brink. I feared the consequences of a public scandal – I was terrified that, if I became involved in action of a legal nature, my wife and my mother might learn of the truth.

But when his note came, accusing me of 'posing' as a sodomite, I knew that I could delay no longer. I sued him for libel. How simple it seems now – and how easy to say that, if I had allowed the matter to pass, similar blows would fall upon me again and again until my position became quite insupportable. But I do not remember thinking of such things at the time. I was lost in an agony of indecision and conflicting emotions, and relied upon the advice of others. I did not wish to 'consider my position', as my friends put it, for it was more dangerous than they knew and I must have suspected even then that any action which I instigated would, inevitably, go against me. And how could it not be so? Perhaps I ran towards my fate, as towards a bride – perhaps I wished to see it clearly for the first time, after the years I had beckoned to it and taunted it. I simply do not know.

Nevertheless, my lawsuit was unforgiveable – the one really foolish action of my life. Instead of mastering life, I allowed it to master me; instead of being the extraordinary dramatist which I was, I became an actor merely, mouthing the lines of others and those which fear and cowardice murmured to me. I let my fate rest in the hands of Society rather than shaping it for myself: I appealed to the very authorities whom I professed to despise. For that I cannot be forgiven, and the memory of my failure haunts me still. It is the reason, I think, why I cannot do the work which I should – the confidence which an artist needs has gone from me. In one fatal minute, in the signing of a piece of paper in a solicitor's office, I abrogated all the responsibilities which attached to me as an artist; and, now, I have inherited only the remains of a personality from which the guiding spirit has fled.

And so I went to trial. But Queensberry's vengeance did not end there: it had a terrible momentum of its own. He had kept in his possession, unknown to anyone, a letter from Rosebery to Drumlanrig – a letter which, as they said of my own at the trials, was 'open to a curious construction'. He had discovered it after Drumlanrig's suicide, and it was his 'trump card', his 'ace' – this was his boast to his family during my imprisonment. After I had been acquitted at my first trial, and he seemed cheated of his prey, Queensberry sent a copy of that letter to someone at the Home Office who knew what might be made of it. He threatened to reveal the letter publicly, unless the authorities continued their prosecution against me in a further trial. Of course they yielded; I became a scapegoat for Rosebery as well as Queensberry's son. I was as a martyr who takes on the responsibilities of an entire Church. That is the truth behind the terrible process I was forced to undergo in the courts.

27 September 1900

I do not wish to enter the *infandum dolorem* of my trial and punishment: when I think of that time, I still experience the strange nausea which affected me then, the sickness which nerves breed. I shall never escape from it: before I eat, I still arrange my cutlery in a precise fashion and become quite unhappy if they are disturbed. That is the legacy of prison. I have visited the Comédie Française only once since my confinement: the three knocks which herald the performance made me utterly distraught and I left the theatre, for it was those three knocks which proclaim the entry of the judge at the Old Bailey. It is foolish of me to behave so, but I have learned that one's own life can become a prison more durable than stones or iron bars. I must close the window: it is growing chilly.

Before the trial of Queensberry on the charge of libelling me, the trial which to my shame and ultimate ruin I myself had caused, I already knew that the gutters of London had been swept by the Marquess and his associates – that they had found some of the boys who had been my companions. My friends earnestly advised me to drop the case and flee the country – and, indeed, my first instinct was to do so. But although I was frightened, mortally frightened, it was fear that gave me strength: the strength to seek an end to it. If I had left the country, that fear would follow me always and I knew what a terrible botch my life would have then become. At least now events have followed their appropriate pattern. To have crossed the Channel to France would have been the act of a coward: I would rather be a byword of infamy for the rest of my days than an object of gross ridicule.

And so, despite my great fear, I stayed. I asked Alfred Taylor to plead with the boys, and to offer them money. But he was being followed continually by two detectives, and could not do so: I did not know then, and the knowledge would have filled me with horror, that a month later we would stand together in the dock. And so I asked Peter Burford to speak to the boys on my behalf, and he tried to do so. He offered them money, and of course they took it. Even empty promises cannot be bought cheaply. He would report to me at Tite Street in his own special language.

'Are you fly to what's going on, Oscar?'

Of course I was, but he expressed it more beautifully than I could.

'They collect the dibs and then they welsh on yer. You've got to be on the q.t. with these pullets.'

I asked him about one particular boy, whose evidence I most feared because of his youth.

'He's off in America gayin' it and flashin' his meat. No worries there.'

I took comfort in small matters of this kind because, in my moments of light-headedness and vanity, I had no doubt about the outcome of the trial. Mrs Robinson had looked at my hand and prophesied success – perhaps success has always been written on my palm, since the gods are noted for their sense of humour. I was confident, also, because I knew precisely what I had to say when I stepped into the witness box. I had rehearsed my answers and my opponent, Edward Carson, had been a particularly dull boy at Trinity. Events conspired to intoxicate me – if more intoxication was needed – and when I entered the courtroom of the Old Bailey it was as if I were going upon a stage. I had been in Washington during the trial of Guiteau, the assassin of President Garfield: he used to sign autographs in the courtroom, and I remember thinking how absurd it was that such a privilege had been denied to my own audience. That it was an audience I was in no doubt: they had come to watch me perform and, I suspect, to forget my lines.

At first I was triumphant. Carson made the mistake of cross-examining me about my own writing – he ought to have known that an artist is his own bitterest accuser, his own most relentless examiner. But Carson tried to take my place: he raised his eyes to Olympus and, bedazzled, tripped and fell. Philistines are uninteresting on the theme of literature simply because they cannot express themselves properly: I have always thought that their views would have a certain charm if they were elegantly phrased. I fully anticipated Carson's line of questioning: I knew that I was to be hounded just as much for my art as for my companions. When Carson read out in his quite exaggerated Irish voice certain passages from a letter I had written to Bosie, the beauty of which survived even his delivery, it was clear that they offended him terribly. And that pleased me: it lent me a certain superiority.

But, when he came to question me about the boys, I faltered. I created a drama in which I figured prominently as a benevolent relation, but, alas, I misjudged the powers of my imagination. I faltered as any artist must when he is forced to walk into the world, especially with a QC as a companion, and to justify himself in the language of the world. Anyone's activities, when read out in open court, would deserve a criminal prosecution on the grounds of banality alone.

Carson mentioned certain names and places. He questioned me about certain gifts I had presented, and was impertinent about my evenings at the lodgings of Alfred Taylor. He hinted at certain 'shocking facts' and, when he informed the jury that the boy I had fondly imagined to be in America was waiting to give evidence, I knew I was lost. I, who had constructed a philosophy out of the denial of conventional reality, found myself impaled upon it. I had always asserted that an interpretation is more interesting than a fact: I was proved unfortunately to be right. I was destroyed by the sordid interpretations which others gave to my affairs: it is amusing, is it not?

I could have fled the country when Sir Edward Clarke gave up my prosecution against Queensberry, and a warrant was issued for my arrest; but I did not do so. I felt myself to be overtaken by events and, in my utter dejection of spirit, I simply did not believe that any action of mine could save me. I had appealed to the world to save my reputation, and it crushed me.

I sat in the Cadogan Hotel on that fatal afternoon, drinking hock-and-seltzer with Bosie. For some reason I took a curious pleasure in reading the early editions of the evening newspapers. The *Echo*, I remember, said that I was 'damned and done for' and I laughed out loud at the phrase; when I read in the *News* that a warrant had been issued against me for 'gross indecency', it was as if that paragraph had been written about someone quite other than myself. I remarked to Bosie at the time that I knew how people loved, but I did not know until then how they could hate. And so I waited for the world to make its next move. It had destroyed my will, my confidence both as a man and as an artist, and it became a matter of relative indifference to me what it did with my body.

At about six o'clock, two detectives entered my room without knocking.

'Mr Wilde, I believe?' one of them said to me.

'If you do not know now, you never will.' I believe I was a little hysterical.

'I must ask you, Mr Wilde, to accompany us to the police station.'

'May I finish my drink?'

'No, sir, you may not.' It was then I realised that my freedom was at an end.

A crowd had gathered outside the hotel. I stumbled on the portal and, as I did so, I heard shouts of, 'Here he is!' They jeered at me as I was led into an ugly vehicle. I was then taken to Bow Street police station, and locked into a cell. I remember nothing of that day, except for the turning of keys and the slamming of doors: it was as if I had entered the Block of Pandemonium. A veil of darkness has settled over those terrible hours and I do not care to pierce it, and see my own face, hear my own words, distorted by fear as they must then have been. I had been waiting for that day all my life – its secrets had been whispered to me in my childish hours and I had seen its image in my dreams.

While I lay in a prison cell, my house was ransacked by creditors, my family forced into hiding, my books and paintings sold. But, in the first days of my imprisonment, I accepted such events without any feelings of a marked kind: there is a limit to the suffering one can impose upon oneself, and I could not have accepted any more without being utterly destroyed. I was beset, instead, by small, pitifully small, anxieties. Instead of concentrating upon the fate of my wife and children, I thought continually of the fact that I had no cigarettes. Instead of concerning myself with my manuscripts, which had passed into the hands of casual buyers, I fretted that I had no books to read in my cell.

But I was more fortunate than I knew. Without books or cigarettes there was nowhere I could find refuge, and so I was forced to look at reality in a different way. The shock of my fall was so great that I became extremely curious about the world which had suddenly been revealed to me, for it seemed to be formed upon principles quite different from those I had imagined. The engine of life was an infernal one, and I was eager to talk to those who, all along, knew this to be so and who acted in accordance with its laws. In the centre of London I was sealed off just as certainly as if I were in a sarcophagus, and I wished to understand the dead who lay there with me. It was, you might say, the beginning of a new life.

28 September 1900

After many days and many nights – I do not remember how many, since time has no meaning for those who are forced to look into their own hearts – I was taken from my cell to the Old Bailey in a closed van. I travelled with other prisoners but, for some reason, I alone was the object of pity. The baths in prison, I was told, were 'fine but 'ot' – if I was fortunate, I would be consigned to Brixton because there were 'a lot of gentlemen' there. One deranged young woman, who had been accused of pick-pocketing in the Strand, showed me a piece of paper on which she had scrawled a speech in her own defence. I advised her not to read it in open court – it was the most damning indictment I have ever read.

We were taken from the van and led down a stone corridor which had arched cells on either side of it – it reminded me rather of the Adelphi. When my name was called, I mounted a flight of wooden stairs and, to my astonishment, found myself in the dock itself. I dislike surprises intensely: I was seized with a fit of violent trembling and could hardly bring myself to look at the faces of those who knew me, and of those who had come to witness my disgrace. And, when the clerk of the court repeated the charges 'against the peace of our Lady the Queen, her Crown and dignity', I felt the chill which only fear can bring. Power has dazzled me always, but never had it seemed more terrible than when I became its catspaw. My friends had told me that I would be able to resume my old life if I left the Old Bailey a vindicated man but I knew that, whatever the verdict, this would be impossible. A whole history of infamy – real or imagined, it was no matter – was to be attached to my name, and I would never be able to free myself from it. I had lived by legend, and I would die by it.

I had not lied to my counsel, Sir Edward Clarke, when I told him on my honour as a gentleman that I was not a sodomite. I had never committed that sin. But truth is the last thing to be

141

discovered in the well of a court: for three days certain boys were paraded in the witness box, much to the delight of the spectators, having been coached in their lies and trained in their accusations against me. I have always worshipped at the altar of the imagination, but I never believed that I would become a sacrifice upon it. I did not lie with Edward Shelley, as time and again he suggested in cross-examination: on the night we spent together, he was so embarrassed by his state of intoxication that I allowed him to stay with me at my hotel rather than return to his parents. It seems that one pays for one's acts of kindness as dearly as one pays for one's sins. When I took Charlie Parker back to the Savoy, it was for Bosie's pleasures and not my own.

I was at first quite composed, since I was convinced that under Sir Edward's interrogation these young men would show themselves to be the perjurers they were – and, indeed, much of their evidence was dismissed. But it soon became clear to me, and to Sir Edward, that the lust for vengeance against me was too strong to be averted. For it is the vengeance wreaked upon those who reach too far – the world holds on to them, and will not let them escape, and I was painted already as a creature of sin, fit only to dwell in the valley of Malebolge with Simon Magus and Bertran de Born.

At first I could not think clearly how to respond. Confinement had coached me in the ways of suffering, and the dock had instilled in me the lessons of fear. And yet, as the recital of imaginary and misattributed crimes continued, an angry will rose up in me just at the moment when my personality seemed quite buried beneath the weight of infamy. In my pride, I saw myself as standing apart – I was being condemned by my inferiors, and I could not allow them to claim their victory without asserting myself as an artist, an artist who was being punished merely because he had the misfortune to be born in the wrong age.

I went into the witness box and refuted all that had been said against me in a clear, calm voice and, as I spoke, I felt triumphant. I made a speech on the nature of Socratic love – I had prepared it in advance – and in a few quiet, simple words I summed up the philosophy of a life-time. These are the words you wish to deny me, I thought, but I will leave them ringing in your ears.

It was that speech, I think, that moved certain jurors and prevented them from condemning me. But I knew that there was to be no victory: I had lied in some parts of my testimony, I admit it, and attempted to conceal much that I was afraid of. I had mixed truth with imagination, and used silver words to conceal the fear and the humiliation which were my constant companions. And they were waiting for me still: as soon as I understood that there was to be a second trial, at the insistence of Queensberry who held the letter from Rosebery like a sword suspended, the confidence which I had momentarily regained deserted me. I was lost.

When I was released on bail, the pursuit began in earnest: I had goaded the monster and it rushed towards me with redoubled steps. I was driven away from the Old Bailey by two friends, but we were followed by Queensberry like a fury. The mob outside the court, cheated of their prey, would have torn me limb from limb; and, where once the streets of London had seemed to me a glorious pageant, now they took on the lineaments of a nightmare. I was hunted by the scarlet Marquess and his gang, and could find no place where they did not follow me and point me out. The hotels which once welcomed me now shut their doors. As I drove through the streets on that evening, searching for a house where I might rest my head, I caught sight of my name on placards and newspaper boys cried it out in the gutters. It was as if I were driving through the landscape of my imagination, full of strange sights and haunted by the voice which calls out 'I! I!' without understanding the meaning of its cry.

And so I fled to my mother's house in Oakley Street. My personality had been stripped from me, piece by piece, and I returned to the terrible nakedness of childhood, alone and afraid. The shock of my fall had destroyed my mother – I saw that at once even through the mist of my misery. She had given me her dreams, and I had shattered them; she had seen in me the best part of herself, and I had betrayed her.

I remained with her for two days, and they were unendurable to me. In her grief, she fell back helplessly upon the life she had known in Ireland. She would talk to me about her childhood in Wexford, laughing all the while, and then her mood would change abruptly and she would complain about her husband's cowardice in not appearing at his own scandalous trial. While I was locked in interviews with my solicitors, she would enter and announce that there was no disgrace for an Irishman to stand in an English dock. She simply did not understand. It was in that dark house that she told me the awful secret of my illegitimacy: the whole pattern of my life became clear then, and I joined hands with my destiny as in a dance of death.

I could not stay with her; each hour heaped a new grief upon my head, and so I travelled secretly to the house of the Leversons.

The Sphinx, in her gentleness of spirit, placed me in her daughter's nursery and there, among the wooden animals and abandoned toys, I understood what a career mine had been. It is possible, in moments of extreme unhappiness, to see one's life from a great height – and I saw mine then. I had been in a nursery always and, like a wilful child, I had smashed and destroyed those things which were dearest and closest to me.

Constance visited me in that house but she hardly dared look at me: I had become monstrous to her. She understood now that she had known nothing about me: I wanted to take her in my arms, but instinctively she shrank back.

'What have you done, Oscar? What have you done?'

'There is no need to sound like a Victorian heroine, my dear.'

She left the room. I do not know why I said it. I simply said it.

Others came to see me – Dowson, Sherard, Harris, all of them begging me once again to flee. But I could not: all flight is the flight away from one's self, and I could never be free of that. Only an artist can understand another artist and, when Lautrec came to paint me, he offered me neither pity nor sympathy; I was grateful for that. He had the clear, dry understanding of one who is an outcast also, since I, like him, now walked as a stranger through the world. I could not admit that to anyone: I could not admit it because I dared not display myself, to those who had known me at the height of my powers, as the miserable and shrunken creature I felt myself to be. And so I hid in the house, preparing a defence which I knew to be worthless.

My final trial took place on Ascension Day – although I, like Don Giovanni, was to travel to a different place. I do not remember the course of that trial now. There are patches of darkness where I see nothing clearly and as for the rest, well, it was terribly familiar. Although the voices rang out in denunciation, I did not understand what was being said: it was as if they were speaking of someone other than myself, someone I would soon have to meet and whose hand was outstretched to greet me and then to pull me down.

As soon as one's personality becomes a matter of public knowledge, and one's history is recited in the form of an indictment, it is remarkable how little hold one retains upon it. I became visibly what others thought, and said, of me: I grew tired, and old. In my last role, in the glare of the public gaze, I gave myself up to the hands of others.

When the verdict of 'guilty' came, it was as if the whole of my life had come to an end. It was a death worse than physical death because I knew that I would survive it and be raised as Lazarus was raised – Lazarus who wept continually after his resurrection because his death was the only real experience he had ever had. The judge uttered those words of condemnation which I had always feared and, in my delirium, I wished to fall in front of the court and confess the sins of my entire life, to utter all the terrible secrets which I harboured and the strange ambitions which I had nourished. I wished to become like a child, and speak simply for the first time. But the judge waved me away, and I was taken in handcuffs to the waiting van.

29 September 1900

I must tell you this fantasy of mine. A young man was wandering through the fields and forests of his native countryside; he was whispering the secrets of his heart to a young girl to whom he was betrothed and, since they were not very profound secrets, she laughed and her laughter rose into the trees.

It was their custom each day to walk to the Grove of Hyacinths, called so because of the richness and profusion of blossoms to be found here – there was a clear pool in the centre of this grove, and they would refresh themselves with its waters. But on this morning, as they entered the place, the young man saw a silver casket, half covered by blossoms.

It had not been there when they had sat and laughed on the previous day and, since this was a sacred place, they decided that the gods must have left it. The young man brushed the fallen hyacinths off the casket, and saw that it was curiously engraved with symbols which he could not decipher. There was no lock upon it and, when he opened the lid, he found within it a hoard of bright coins – more coins that he had seen in his entire life. On the face of each coin there was the face of a strange king: a tired, old face with no name inscribed beneath it. And the young girl was bewildered: 'There is something of evil about that face,' she said, 'let us leave the coins and return to our village. For look, the sun is immediately above our heads and I must prepare the meal for those returning from the fields.' But the young man paid no heed to her: 'Look how the sun makes these coins wink and glow,' he said. 'Surely these are precious coins, and we will live in riches for the rest of our lives.' For the young man was poor, and often slept beneath the sky when he could not afford shelter. And he would not be persuaded to leave the coins.

So the young girl returned home, alone and sorrowful, while the young man journeyed with the casket to the great city which was the centre of his region. He went into the market of the city and approached a merchant of cloth: 'I wish to buy a fine cloak, with the purple which comes from Tyre and the silk which comes from Chalcedon.' The merchant laughed at him, and asked how he could afford such a cloak. And the young man showed him some of the coins which he had found in the Grove of Hyacinths. The merchant looked upon them and laughed at him again. 'These coins are counterfeit coins. They are worthless here. Get you gone before the guards with their burnished swords arrest you.' And the young man grew afraid, and moved on. He went to the merchant who sold sweetmeats, and said to him, 'I wish to buy those sweetmeats which are made on the banks of the Tigris, and of which one taste is sufficient to show strange visions.' And the merchant looked at him with scorn, and demanded how he would pay for such things. The young man showed him the coins and the merchant grew more scornful still. 'These are not real coins,' he said. 'There is no king in this land who resembles the king upon the coins. Get you gone before I proclaim your villainy in the Place of Accusation.' And the young man departed in great uncertainty of mind.

But, as he left the market place, he passed the temple, and he went inside the temple and laid the casket of coins before the altar of the one-eyed god as an offering. But a priest hurried towards him, and questioned him. 'I am leaving these coins here,' he said, 'to placate the god in whose eye we live.' And the priest examined the coins, and then put his robe before his face. 'I have seen these coins before,' he whispered, 'and they bring evil with them. Get you gone before I charge you with sacrilege in the temple.'

And the young man fled from the city weeping but, as is often the case with young men, his sorrow soon turned to bitterness and anger. He returned to his native village and went to the house of the girl to whom he was betrothed. 'These coins have brought contempt and ill fortune upon me,' he said, 'and I must needs find the king whose face is upon them, and him will I slay.' The girl begged him to forget his foolish vengeance, but he would not listen to her and left her to her tears. The birds in the trees heard their conversation, and they sang to each other: 'Why is he becoming so angry? They are only pieces of metal.' And the flowers had heard also, and whispered to each other, 'Why does he concern himself with such things? We flourish, and have no need of money.'

And so the young man began his journey. He travelled to the kingdom of perpetual snow where there is no word for the sun; he travelled to the kingdom of the cave-dwellers whose bodies are as transparent as soft gauze; he travelled to the desert region where the sun is so bright that night never descends and the eyes of the old men are blind. And in each place they threw the coins in his face, for they had no such king.

He journeyed to the City of the Seven Sins, where young men touched him and whispered among themselves. But the prophet who lived in that city begged him to turn back: his search was futile, he said, and would be terrible for him. But he heeded him not. He visited the wise woman who sings to the bones in the Valley of Desolation, and when she saw him she laughed a fearful laugh. She prophesied that, if he found the object of his quest, then the king would surely slay him. But he grew wroth, and turned her aside with bitter words. He travelled to the Mountains of Desire where the wind speaks through the stones; he called out his question, 'Where will I find the king whom I seek?' And the stones answered him: 'He is more distant than the most distant star, and he is closer than your eye.' He wondered and understood not, and so he journeyed onward to the barren land where only the great statue of the Hippogriff stands. And he asked the statue to unravel the meaning of the stones, and the Hippogriff gave answer that there were some secrets which might never be divulged.

At the end of many years of barren journeying, the man returned, sorrowful and resentful, to his own land. By chance he entered the Grove of Hyacinths on his way back to the village and there, sitting by the clear pool in the centre of the Grove, was an old woman. She looked at him in wonder, and her wonder was mixed with tears. 'Why are you so tired and worn?' she asked him. 'When you left this place, you were as handsome as the bright day.' For in truth the old woman was that girl whom he had once promised to marry. 'I have spent my life in weary wandering,' he replied to her, 'for I have been seeking the king whose face marks the coins I found in this accursed place, so that I might kill him.' And in his grief he threw the coins upon the ground. The old woman picked up one of the coins, and gazed upon the face of the king. When she saw that face, she ran away, weeping. 'Why do you run from me?' he called out to her and, as she ran, she cried, 'It is your own face I see upon the coins.' And he looked at them and there, in the face of the king, a restless and tired face, with something of evil in it, was his own face. It was his own face stamped upon the counterfeit coins. And he took out his sword and fell upon it.

4 October 1900

After my conviction I was driven in a prison van to Pentonville. My hair was cut so short that I resembled a philanthropist, my clothes and my possessions were roughly taken from me, and I put on the coarse brown and black prison dress with its arrows – I would rather that each arrow had pierced me than wear the ill-fitting garb which gave sorrow a clownish face, and redoubled pain with the crude symbols of guilt. Then boots were thrown in the middle of the vast reception room – and those of us who had lately come were forced to scramble for them.

I was addressed in a quite anonymous fashion: I had been 'sent out' and now I was 'received': really, I might have been a parcel. A letter was chalked upon the back of my prison dress, and I was led through the metal corridors of Pentonville. I was then placed in a cell, where a clergyman of vicious aspect came to catechise me. He left two pamphlets which I was to read, over and over again, in the months that followed: 'The Converted Charwoman of Goswell Road' – her case was of particular interest – and 'How are Your Poor Fingers, you Blackguard?' This was a gloating account of the picking of oakum, which rivalled even the modern novel in its inability to understand suffering.

A schoolmaster visited my cell immediately after the clergyman. He asked me if I could read – I told him that I could not remember – and how I spelled 'oxen'. I submitted to this meekly, for in truth I felt nothing. I was in the trance that follows delirium: if I had been under the surgeon's knife, I would not have cried out. During that first night, life and sensation returned slowly back to me – the horror of it remains with me still, for life returned in the form of fear. I understood what had happened to me, but it was only then that I began to experience it; the awful stench of prison, the flickering half-light from the gas jet outside my cell, and the silence which of all things marks the dead and the dying, all these rose up and stifled me. I was afraid to cry out, terrified even to move from the wooden plank which bore my weight. If someone then had asked me who I was, I would have known how to answer: I was the stench, I was the half-light and I was the silence. For three days and three nights, nausea overwhelmed and, when I placed my head in the bucket, it was as if I was expelling all of my old life. That is why I no longer care to recover my old personality now and why, to the astonishment of my friends, I am content to find companions where I may and to talk to those who will listen: what personality I had before was weaker and more ignominious still, for it was stripped from me between one day and the next.

I see my cell clearly still, more clearly than I see this room. There was of course a Bible and a prayer book, and a whole range of common articles for daily use: a tin mug, a tin plate and a tin knife, a box of salt and a small piece of soap. On the plain wooden shelf beside my cell door were two blankets and, in the opposite corner beneath the barred window, were a basin, a slop-pail and a can of water. Outside my cell door was a card on which had been written my name and the particulars of my sentence: everyone knew who I was and what I was there for. Here are the ingredients of a life of penance and meditation, are there not?

My new life was one of barren tasks, tasks which I performed without thought but not without feeling. I stitched canvas sacks for the Post Office, and my fingers bled so that I could scarcely touch anything – the lot of the prisoner will be improved immensely if the telephone becomes fashionable. It seemed to me in those first weeks and months that the world I had known outside my prison cell was a fantastic world of dreams, that it had been an illusion as cunningly wrought as the shadows with whom Faust dances before he is led to perdition. And when I left the prison in order to be examined in the Bankruptcy Court, where I confessed the profligacy of my previous life, I felt an unaccustomed shame – not because I was forced to expose my life to common men, but rather because I had deceived myself in my extravagance. My examiners knew far more of the world than I did – after all, it had been fashioned in their image – and I was like a child being called to account.

But since I had been stripped of my personality, as a result I became pathetically grateful to any who looked on me with kindly eye or spoke words of comfort to me. Once when we trudged around the yard, with three paces between each man, a prisoner muttered brief words to cheer me. I was not skilled in the ways of concealment and, when I returned his kindness, with tears in my eyes, I was overheard. For that brief moment of companionship, I was brought up before the governor of the prison and sentenced to three days' solitary confinement in the 'punishment cell'.

It was a fiendish place, fitted with double doors so that no sound came from without, furnished only with a plank and a stool. Here I was forced to live on stale bread and the brackish water made salt by my tears. In that cell, the effects of gloom, silence and darkness are quite indescribable. I thought I would go mad. I became a victim of the most terrible hallucinations. A spider wove a perilous web in the corner of the cell and, when I peered at it, I saw my own face staring back at me. The patchwork of lines upon the walls formed fetid shapes of lust, and I began to dwell at length on the sins of my past and to dream of fresh sins so vivid that I hid myself from them, and wept. And then in the silence, a silence broken only by the wind, I would talk to myself. I held conversations in which I laughed at my own wit. I paced up and down the narrow confines of that dark place and, in grotesque parody of my former life, would strike attitudes and converse with the spider who watched me with unblinking eyes.

The image of those three days and three nights has never left me; sometimes now, in the middle of a conversation, I remember my dialogue with the spider and am struck dumb. That is why I cannot bear to be alone: solitude frightens me because it seems to me to be the simplest thing to slip back into a dementia from which I would never be able to free myself. It is the fear of solitude which makes me write now: if I closed this book and put down my pen, I would become a prey again to all those horrors which, since they spring from myself, cannot be turned aside.

I bear, also, the physical marks of that solitary confinement. One night, I awoke suddenly from sleep and my mother stood beside me. I rose from my bed, but I could not speak – she lifted her arm, as if to strike me, and with a cry of terror I fell back upon the floor and knocked my ear against the plank bed. No, that is not right. I fell upon the ground in the exercise yard. Have I not described this already?

I am told now that I have so severely damaged my ear that deafness is inevitable. That is why I have these pains in my head and why each morning I find my pillow stained with the yellow mucus. I see again my mother with her hand raised against me, and the same terror fills me. I feel myself falling upon the stony ground of the yard, and I am in pain. Which is the truth – will it be pain or fear that destroys me?

The doctors in Pentonville, who would have been more usefully employed in an abattoir, came to examine me. There had been reports in the press that I had become insane: gleeful reports, since men enjoy tasting the fruits sown in blood. But I would surely have died if I had remained in that place, and the authorities wished to avoid an early martyrdom. And so the doctors recommended that I be sent to a prison 'in the country'.

In obedience to their commands, I was taken in a chain gang to Reading. At each station we were hooted at and, on one platform where we were forced to alight, I was surrounded by a mob who recognised me; a man spat in my face. I had not known what human beings were like until I stood among them manacled: I longed for confinement then. Jesus only found rest from his tormentors in the tomb: I did not find it until I entered the gates of prison.

When we arrived at Reading station, I could see the elaborate arches and ornate carvings which I had once known so well: it seemed unimaginative of the railway authorities that they should be there still when I had changed in so grotesque a fashion. For I had passed that station many times on my way to Oxford, although in those days it had not been a station of the cross. While we were marched into a waiting van, I reflected on the quite painful change in my condition and yet it was the philosophy which I learned at Oxford which had brought me to this point. I had affirmed the values of the individual personality: my age had flung those values back into my face. And my days in the darkened cell had shown me what I really was.

Other men find strength in prison or, if they do not find strength, at least they find faith. But I had found nothing within myself: I saw now quite clearly that I had no real values of my own except those which others had bequeathed to me. I was like a man standing on the edge of a cliff: from afar he looks glorious but, if you were to approach him, you would see that his eyes are closed so that he might not see the emptiness beneath him. And of course he falls.

I had not known the world as it really is. I ignored suffering. I chose not to see it. My good nature was a form of complacency and

153

of cowardice: I did not want to be moved by any single emotion in case I was overwhelmed by them all. I was afraid of passion – real passion – since I did not know what it might reveal of me, both to myself and to others. And yet passion, the passion of sorrow wrenched out of my mouth at the sight of doom, had lain in wait for me; it was the thread of my life which I had now to gather up. And, when the chain gang alighted at the gates of Reading prison, I knew I must find it there.

Intentions are of no importance, however, if the capacity to fulfil them does not exist. And my first few months in Reading were very hard. The governor there was a foolish man, a mere emblem of officialism. His régime spread throughout the entire prison, so that one's life was brutalised by tyrannous regulations where it was not trivialised by petty restrictions. Because of the nature of my crimes he placed me under 'special observation' in my first months. Every half-hour a warder would look in upon me – I could hear his footsteps and then, when I glanced up, I would see his solitary eye peering through the glass spyhole in the door of my cell: I knew then how Odysseus felt in the cave of Cyclops.

It pleased this governor to allot as one of my tasks the cleaning of the scaffold – and, indeed, I was curious to see it, with the curiosity of those who have abandoned all higher feeling. It had been constructed in a little wooden shed in a corner of the prison yard which, in my innocence, I had thought to be a greenhouse. It was my task to scrub the wooden flooring of this place, and on my first visit it was pointed out to me by the cheerful warder who watched my labours that the solid floor itself gave way to a bricked pit below. In his enthusiasm, he cranked the wheel and a long bolt forced the floor apart: to launch the victim into mid-air. And there was the pit. I felt dizzy, as if there had been no bottom to it. And, indeed, where death has been there is only an airless void in which the body, pinioned and silent, falls. The warder laughed at my distress, and made as if to push me into it. It was then that I was sick, violently sick, and the warder redoubled his laughter. This is what men do to each other when all pity has fled.

During those first months in Reading I was helpless, quite helpless. All I could do was weep, wrack my body with the rage I could not otherwise express and which I turned against myself in the guise of pain. My eyesight began to fail, from the strain of picking oakum in my cell, and because of the injury to my ear my hearing began to fail also. In my state of nervous hysteria, I thought I would go mad. Indeed I grew half in love with madness – I saw nothing else for me which would release me from my sufferings.

Two friends were allowed to visit me once in every three months and, although those who made the pilgrimage thought that they were assisting me, I found in such encounters only further humiliation. I would be placed in a cage with wire netting in front of it, and they would sit in a hutch of similar construction; there was a narrow corridor between us along which the warder trod. Of course conversation of any kind was impossible – there were four such cages on either side, and the babble of voices was indescribable.

I was ashamed, also, of my physical appearance – I was not allowed to shave, and my face was thick with stubble. One cannot say anything without the proper clothes, and in the dress of a convict I spoke very little. Sometimes, in my distress, I would place a handkerchief over my face in order to hide myself from the eyes of even those whom I knew best. And they had, for their part, very little to say to me – they came, after all, from a world which had condemned me and left me to die in solitude.

'How are you, Oscar?' More asked on the occasion of his visit.

'I am very well. Can you not see?' There was a silence.

'Well, take heart.'

'May I ask why?'

'We are organising a petition on your behalf. Frank is to see the Home Secretary next week.'

'I am the most famous prisoner in England, am I not? How are my sons?'

'They are well, and Constance is well also.'

'Do they ask after me?'

'Of course.'

'And do they know where I am?'

'They believe you to be in hospital.'

'It will be a very long illness, I'm afraid. More, I want you to be a dear kind fellow and do something for me. I wish you to visit Constance in Italy – do not write, she is frightened of letters now – and ask her simply and plainly if she means to support me after I leave this place. I merely wish to know.'

'Could you not leave all this for a few months, Oscar. You know that Constance has made herself quite ill with anxiety –'

'No. I must know now. The idea of poverty torments me, More.

You talk of Constance, but can you imagine what I suffer –'

The warder then came between us, and I was taken back to my cell.

It was my wife who saved me from the torment which I thought would last for ever. She travelled from Genoa, where she had hurried with our children into exile, in order to tell me of the death of my mother. She did not wish me to hear that news from the lips of those who did not care for me. For the first time I wept in front of her: my mother's death was a blow insupportable to me. Constance wept also, with a grief as great as mine, and in that exchange of woe I sensed dimly the one thing that might save me. For when I shared my suffering with Constance, I saw it as something quite outside myself. What touched my heart had touched Constance's also, and I began to understand that I might endure my own pain, as she endured hers, in sympathy with the pain of others. If I was as greedy with my sufferings as I had been with my pleasures, then surely I would be lost.

Across the landing from my cell, a young boy had been incarcerated for a petty theft. When I returned from the interview with Constance, I could hear him weeping, and now I could weep with him – the first tears I had not shed for myself alone, tears which carried me forward until I saw life plainly. The shock of my mother's death opened my eyes to the suffering of others. There was a madman, King, who was continually being flogged for his gibberings and his insane laughter. We could all hear his screams, but, where before I had understood them only as an echo of my own anguish, I saw now that the terror of his own life was greater than my own. Why had I not known it before, when others knew it? I sat on my plank and laughed out loud at my own blindness.

I realised that I had seen life through my intelligence, and through the pride which springs from intelligence, not through the emotions which now shook me and which I endured willingly for the first time. In my grief, I had once looked to find death, and now I was learning to see life, what Carlyle calls somewhere 'the temple of immensity'. Sorrow taught me how to sit and look. Pity taught me to understand. Love taught me to forgive.

And then the miracle occurred, the miracle which love needs in order to blossom. A new governor took the place of him whose régime might have destroyed me – Major Nelson, a kind, patient man, arrived and at once the atmosphere of Reading changed for all its prisoners. It was my psychological moment: my fall had broken me apart, and I was ready to receive those new and sweeter impressions with which I might begin to rebuild my life.

Nelson allowed me books, and I began haltingly to read. I felt nothing for literature at the beginning: all words seemed dead to me, and injurious also, for they lead men where they should not go. I was given 'improving' literature, however – with the possible exception of Emerson's essays – and I sat down humbly with it, as if I were a child. I began with the simple Latin of St Augustine. Then I read Dante and walked with him in the Purgatory which I had known before, but which now I saw in the light of understanding. I was given a volume of Aeschylus, and I fell again under the spell of ancient things: the prison shades fell away and I was standing in the clear, bright air. The texture of language itself, like the veil of Tannith in Flaubert's delicate novel, clung about me and protected me. I called upon Dionysus, the loosener of lips and of the heart, and his splendour interposed between me and the darkness so that I was at once revivified and joyful.

Yes, it is curious – one can experience joy in a prison cell, for I had found that within me which had survived my bitterness and my humiliation. It was then that I determined upon artistic work again. The governor allowed me certain writing materials, and at night I would work beneath a single gas lamp in my cell. At first I could make notes on my reading only: I did not trust myself with the words I had once used too freely. But I knew that other artists had found in suffering the one perfect subject and I began actively to plan, once my term of imprisonment had drawn to its close, the lineaments of a new art that I would create from my pain as a bronze figure is fashioned from the fire. There were two trees just beyond the prison wall – I could glimpse them from my cell, and through the winter I had watched their long, black branches through which the wind sighed as though its heart was broken. Now, in the spring, they began to blossom. I knew exactly what they were experiencing: they were finding expression.

A new warder, Thomas Martin, took charge of my landing: his cheerfulness and kindness strengthened my resolve to free myself from the pit into which I had been flung. He would smuggle biscuits and newspapers to me, although I believe the biscuits were of a more sensational character. Such small acts of kindness are greater than the blessings of the gods, for the gods do not understand men and offer that which we do not need.

Tommy was a young man of impressive appearance but also of impeccable morals. After we had been in each other's company for several weeks, he asked me about my relations with the boys who had appeared at my trials. He asked me, with all the curiosity of a thoroughly disinterested person, what I did with them.

'I kissed them all over their bodies.'

'Why?'

'What else is there to do with a charming young man except kiss him?'

'I hope you washed them first.'

'When the Athenians were sent children from the Gods, Tommy, they honoured them. They did not enquire in a Fabian manner into their domestic circumstances.'

He left me contrite, but fortunately he remembered to remove my pail.

I asked Tommy if he had heard of me even before my trials, and invited him to speculate on the extent of my fame among the working classes – the answers were most satisfactory. And, since he knew of my connection with literature, Tommy asked me to solve newspaper competitions for him and other warders. I contrived slogans to win sets of china. 'They would suit us to a tea,' I wrote in a poetical moment. 'A tea service is the *grounds* of a good marriage.' They were my Fleet Street eclogues, and indeed such competitions comprise the only value I have ever seen in the daily press.

By the spring of 1897, I had spent almost two years in prison. I was forty-two years old. As the moment of my release came nearer, I grew nervous of what might greet me when I left Reading. My financial affairs had been grotesquely mismanaged by my friends: promises had been broken, and I knew that I would leave prison as a pauper. I quite seriously considered beginning my new life as a vagrant, until I remembered that such a life had already become a cliché of modern literature. No, it was not for me to bow my head before the world. I could not allow my accusers to say that they had destroyed me: I would have to rise above them, unaided. I alone had to decide the nature of my new life; I would have to remake myself as an artist for, if I failed, I would mar myself still further as a man. It was a terrible course, but only because I did not know if I had the strength to pursue it.

On the day I left Reading, I was handed the clothes which I had worn when I first entered prison. They were of course too large for me now, and they smelled somewhat of disinfectant as if they had been used to wrap a corpse. A half-guinea was given to me in payment for two years' labour – the last money I have ever earned.

I shook hands with the governor, and turned to Tommy Martin who stood by my side. He was smiling, and I broke into laughter. 'Think of me sometimes,' I said to him: I believe he does, just as I often remember him and his kindness which restored life to me. I walked out from the gates of Reading prison, and looked up at the sky. I was taken on a train to Pentonville, and then I was released to my friends in London.

6 October 1900

I was so pleased with my account of life in prison, with the pearl I had created out of two years' suffering, that I took this journal with me when I went to lunch with Bosie at the Richaux. I saw Frank Harris there and asked him to join us – on the principle that if Frank is not with you he is against you. At first I kept the book mysteriously by my side, but the suspense grew too much for me and I placed it upon the table.

'What is that, Oscar, a ledger of debts?'

'Yes, Bosie, it is. But they are not debts which money could repay.'

'Your debts never are.' This, of course, was Frank.

'I will read you a passage, Frank, if you will allow an artistic note to be introduced into our conversation.'

I think I recited to them the pages concerning my triumphant days in London society. They were astonished, naturally, and took the book from me. They read it, practically arm in arm, while I gazed out of the window. Eventually, Frank looked up at me.

'You cannot publish this, Oscar. It is nonsense – and most of it is quite untrue.'

'What on earth do you mean?'

'It is invented.'

'It is my life.'

'But you have quite obviously changed the facts to suit your own purpose.'

'I have no purpose, and the facts came quite naturally to me.'

'There was a time when you distrusted nature, and rightly so. For example, "in the little theatre in King Street, the young men wore green carnations". Oscar, you were the only person who wore a green carnation. And this, "I was vain and the world loved my vanity". Nobody loved your vanity, Oscar. Surely you know that by now.'

'Don't be so ridiculous, Frank. You are behaving like a weekly reviewer.'

'And you have stolen lines from other writers. Listen to this one—'

'I did not steal them. I rescued them.'

Bosie remained silent: he was biting his fingernails, which is always a sign that he has nothing to say. And so I challenged him.

'And what do *you* think?'

'It's full of lies, but of course you are. It is absurd and mean and foolish. But then you are. Of course you must publish it.'

Frank then continued in the most boring detail about what he called my errors of fact and judgment. I cannot remember them now. I rescued the book from him after some minutes, and asked him to order me a cab.

'Lose the book,' he said, 'for your sake.' Of course I ignored him.

8 October 1900

Prison breeds strange vices: one is the illusion that one deserves to be in such a place, that one belongs as a blind, underground creature might to that world of silence and darkness. When I walked out of prison, the sky dazzled me and I was afraid of falling: for the first time in my life, the world seemed to me to be too large a place. I travelled in a closed carriage from Pentonville to Bloomsbury on that first morning and, while resting in the house of a friend, I wrote a letter to Farm Street couched in terms of humility and sorrow, asking if I might go into retreat.

It seems inconceivable now to me that I should have done so, although I have always had a great affection for the Pope. Perhaps the sight of modern London prompted me to return at once to the safety of a cell, and perhaps I wished to study there the mysteries of love and suffering which had been revealed to me – I do not know, I cannot remember. But my request was refused.

And so I was compelled to face my life, to give it direction and purpose on an alien shore. I crossed to Dieppe on the ferry in the late afternoon and, as I saw the shabby coast of England receding, I felt much like Captain Nemo on board the ship which will take him eternally away from the sight of men. England was never to see me again.

I travelled to Berneval in the first stage of my exile. I took the precaution of doing so under a false name – Sebastian Melmoth, the name by which I am still known to tradespeople. I was free, I quite understood that, but freedom is a curious thing: when one has it, one can think of nothing whatever to do. The sky, the sea, and the simple countryside of Normandy were enchanting, but they lacked the capacity of surprise. I knew that the world should be for me a joyful place, but the secret of that joy was still locked within my breast; I was dazzled by life as if by a grand house – but I was a guest, no longer master.

People visited me in order to see if I had survived the penny papers. They were curious to know if I had changed. I believe I had, although I took care not to show it. Since of all things affection and laughter were precious to me, I did not want to lose them by showing the convict arrows that still pierced my heart. The kindness of others affected me very much, and yet it also exhausted me. Once I had enjoyed being the perpetual object of display, but what had been before an advanced personality was now something of a mannerism. And how could it have been otherwise? In my cell I had seen what a scintillating effect that personality had had upon me: it had almost led me to the lunatic asylum.

But if I could not yet redeem myself, if I was in effect 'lost property' still, I could at least assert myself as an artist. I began writing *The Ballad of Reading Gaol* as soon as I was settled in a small hotel in Berneval. I wanted to demonstrate to English society that it had not destroyed me as an artist, that by some strange paradox it had only provided me with fresh materials for my art. I refused to play the part of a reformed convict: I remember one of the prisoners in Reading, Arthur Cruttenden, saying once of the world that we had left behind, 'Damn the whole boiling of them,' and the phrase had stayed in my mind. It was what I felt but had not yet expressed: my poem would be the only revenge I could take, but it was a glorious one. I wished to show to those people who had convicted me what a world they had constructed; and how I, whose art had been devoted to exposing their follies, had witnessed the ultimate shame and folly of which they were capable.

This pleased me, and in the first weeks of my liberty I was as happy as I have ever been. I wrote, I took reasonably long walks, I bathed daily and, like Aphrodite, I renewed my virginity in the sea. And then, when my friends left me to return to their own lives and my own inspiration began to fail, I became disconsolate again. The shock of my freedom had released in me one great poem, just as it had released a first wild joy, but, alone, I felt the shades of the prison house closing around me again – not the prison which others had constructed for me, but that which I had fashioned for myself.

The life I had once known was gone, and I did not feel that I was capable of renewing it. I began to realise, by slow degrees, what I had known in the year before I was sent to prison: I had died as an artist. *The Ballad* had been wrenched from me as a cry from a wounded animal but, once the pain was gone, I was left with nothing to express. I toyed with the idea of writing religious drama, but I had no stomach for it. I felt that I could do little with my life except drift with it until it ran into the sands. One never leaves prison. Every convict knows that. One merely relives the memory of it.

And so it was that I went back to Bosie: I had no one else to turn to. My wife had quite properly left me, my children were living under another name, and the friends of my infamous years were, as theatrical agents say, 'not available'. Of course I knew Bosie was ruinous for me, but I believe that even Jesus was in league with Judas to hasten his own death . Robbie Ross wrote me a pained letter telling me that it was a great mistake to 'resume relations', as he put it, with 'that young man', but I sent him a telegram: THOSE CAPABLE OF GREAT DEEDS ARE ALLOWED TO COMMIT GREAT ERRORS.

Bosie and I travelled to Naples together: really, I could have written a Neapolitan Tragedy. We trudged in the yard of our doomed friendship like condemned men. And then, quite without warning, Bosie left me. His mother had threatened to cut off his allowance if he remained with me and although he loved the poor, at least in Naples, he did not love poverty. I was alone once more, and solitude reduced me to a shadow. The merest shock would unnerve me; I felt sensitive to every slight, and I would write long but hasty letters insulting those who loved me and attacking those who tried to help. Why do you not send money, I would write, why do you spread false rumours about me in London clubs, what has happened to my *Ballad*?

My life was insupportable alone, and so I made my way here in weariness and in pain. I have always been a part of great cities – I am, after all, a monument now to the grosser aspects of urban civilisation – and, where I had lived, I wanted to die. Like Villon and Baudelaire, my home is the 'paysage de métal et de pierre'. And so for the last two years my life has been as it is now: a mathematical problem rather than a romantic one. I have had to beg for every penny I have. My clothes are positively Norwegian in their shabbiness: I have become like an elderly but amusing aunt. It is strange how people treat me now – they confide in me, where once they simply listened. They know I cannot be shocked, but they also believe that I cannot be bored.

Frank Harris even took me with him to Cannes so that I might listen to him composing – they ought to build a stadium for that man. And, last spring, Harold Mellors journeyed with me to Rome. He paid, of course. And, although I do not care for Mellors, I wished to see the Pope. God went to so much trouble to make St Augustine a bishop, at least according to St Augustine, that I thought he might spare time for my own conversion. I had considered a death-bed repentance but rejected it as too predictable under the circumstances. I always prefer to settle such matters in advance.

I saw the Pope – indeed, I think he saw me first – and then the miracle occurred. My umbrella did not blossom as I had been led to expect, but in that damp and cavernous cathedral, filled with the chant of Easter pilgrims, the entire shape of my life became clear to me. I realised then that I could not have escaped my destiny, and that it was necessary that I should be destroyed before I was permitted to rise again: now I can look death in the face. But I did not become a Christian. In the face of death, I have become a pantheist, polytheist and atheist all at once. I gather all the gods about me because I believe in none. That is the secret of classical civilisation: in Thermopylae, behind the temple of Hercules, there is an altar erected to Pity – and it is there that I prostrate myself still.

And indeed I am quite recovered. If my first year of liberty was a burden to me, it was because I tried to place my old life upon my back and, naturally, I fell beneath its weight. But all that has gone: I have left my art, and I have outgrown the personality which I constructed with it. Now I stand still and wonder at the inexhaustible fullness of things which before I tried to master and control. Napoleon said that 'deep tragedy is the school of great men' and I have realised that for myself at last – what I created was nothing, less than nothing, in the face of the mystery of life. Only in the individual, as poor and as helpless even as I am, and in the mystery of individual lives, is meaning to be found. Life, and the current of life, survives everything. It is greater than myself and yet, without me, it would be incomplete: that is the real miracle.

I was again in great pain this morning and, since my room sometimes has the atmosphere of a tomb, I walked out into the Rue des Beaux Arts – slowly now, with difficulty, but with a sense of wonder. There was a boy playing beside an old accordionist on the corner of the Rue Jacob; he picked up the few sous tossed at

165

the old man, and placed them painstakingly beside him. Just across the street, an old woman was being helped up the stairs of her house by two young men who supported her – there was such gaiety in their faces that the load on my own heart was lightened. A boy patted fondly his dog, which had put its paws on his shoulders. In such details does my mind and heart now dwell. On this day, the eighth of October, 1900, such things will last for ever.

9 October 1900

Here is an extraordinary thing. I was walking by the Seine this morning, when a young couple approached me. I am always wary of such encounters, and I watched them with a cold eye as they came up to me.

'Do I 'ave the pleasure of seeing Mr Oscar Wilde?' the young man said to me. I told him the pleasure was all mine.

'I just want to shake your 'and, Mr Wilde,' he said. His wife kept on opening and closing her eyes, as if the sight was too much for her.

'Well, Mr Wilde, we've read all about your misfortunate time, 'aven't we, Margaret? But are you 'appy now, 'ave you become more like your old self?'

They were goodhearted people, and I told them I was much recovered.

'It was a terrible thing what they did to yer.'

'You meant no 'arm,' the wife said quite suddenly.

'And a writing chap like you needs 'is bit of fun, don't he?'

It was difficult to disagree with the young man and, in any event, he had a charming and obviously new moustache.

'That's what we said at the time, didn't we, Margaret?' His wife batted her eyelids again. 'There was no end of a lot of trouble about yer in the pub, Mr Wilde. Do you 'appen to know the Globe in Forest Hill?'

I said that I could not place it quite.

'We 'ad a good old argument about you there, didn't we, Margaret? Some of them said they should 'ave 'anged yer, but I stuck to me guns. I said to 'em, I said, "'E's done no 'arm. What 'arm's 'e done?" Most of us there were on your side if the truth be known, Mr Wilde. We couldn't see the sense of 'ounding yer. I said to 'em, "What's 'e done which thousands ain't?" And they 'ad to agree, didn't they?'

I was delighted. I could have spent the entire morning discussing my martyrdom with them, but they were in Paris only for a short time and wished to see the other sights. The young man shook me warmly by the hand, and his wife brandished a copy of a women's magazine and asked me if I would very kindly sign it for her.

'Good luck to yer, Mr Wilde,' he said as we parted, 'and may I wish yer 'appy days and many of 'em.' I was deeply touched and I watched them as they walked together, arm in arm, along the Seine. I would have given anything, at that moment, to have been that young woman.

10 October 1900

Robert Ross has sent me a parcel. I opened it in haste, only to discover some copies of *An Ideal Husband*. I had been hoping for jars of Koko-Marikopas, which turns my hair strangely brown. Well, I glanced at the play: I was curious to see what I had written and, with the exception of one or two of the more serious speeches, it amuses me still. But I cannot go back to that kind of thing: unlike Sarah Bernhardt, I cannot be forever striking attitudes. And how can a man, who simply looks at the world and wonders, produce art? It is a thing quite impossible.

Charles Wyndham wrote to me the other day asking me to translate Scribe for a publisher in Bond Street; fortunately, he offered money in advance. I accepted that, of course, but I do not think I can bear to do the translation: I would rather be stitching sacks. Scribe does not write, he tinkers. Only Hugo and Maeterlinck were my equal as dramatists and, in any case, translation is not my *forte*. Like prayer, one should do it in the privacy of one's own home, preferably not aloud.

My career as an artist is complete, and it would be superfluous to attempt to add to it. I went from poetry to prose, and then to drama. After that, I went to prison. There, in two sentences, is the secret of my extraordinary life: always do the unexpected. People rarely forgive you for it, but they never forget you. It was fitting, however, that my last published work should be the *Ballad* and that I should end, as I began, with poetry. Like the head of Orpheus, I sang as I floated into oblivion. I began with the song of Apollo, and ended with the cry of Marsyas.

There have been absurd rumours that I am still writing under an assumed name. Frank Harris told me at lunch – did I mention that lunch? – that *Mr and Mrs Daventry* is about to open at the Royalty: well, royalty devised it. He told me that I am reported to be the author of the play and, although he is the author himself, he

169

laughed at the idea. It will bring the play publicity, he said. But the idea fills me with horror. I devised the scenario, and out of it I could have created a perfect example of domestic melodrama. Frank, however, has taken the thing seriously and written a perfectly dreadful tragedy. If my name is attached to it, it will add yet another chapter to my martyrdom. I believe it is called a 'problem play', although the only real problem is why Frank wrote it. He is not a dramatist: he has no interest in himself, let alone in other people.

Actually, I do not care any more about such matters, although I pretend to do so. Once it was quite otherwise: I laughed about my work with others, and made light of it in conversation with friends, while in reality I thought nothing else to be of the slightest importance. I do not believe that any of my companions realised how serious an artist I then was: when my work touched upon suffering as well as joy, sin as well as love, I was reproached by some of them for being morbid. They wanted me to be always as I seemed to be with them, and it came as a positive disappointment that I might be different out of their company.

I was the greatest artist of my time, I do not doubt that, just as my tragedy was the greatest of its time. I had a reputation as an artist both in Europe and in America, and in England my work was always a commercial success – I am not ashamed of that. The cult of the artist as St Francis has never appealed to me: their virginity is the virginity of the eunuch, their isolation that of the thoroughly understood.

I mastered each literary form. I brought comedy back to the English stage, I created symbolic drama in our tongue, and I invented the prose poem for a modern audience. I divorced criticism from practice, and turned into an independent enquiry, just as I wrote the only modern novel in English. And, although I turned my plays into an essentially private form of expression, I never swerved from my ideal which was to make drama the meeting place of life and art. I proposed a novel theory in doing so: that Man is, or should be, what he appears to be. The public did not understand that, but then the public never understands anything. The problem with the modern age is that it has the merits of chiaroscuro only – with much shade and little light. I reversed the equation and the public were dazzled.

Of course there were great faults, but if there had been no faults there would have been no triumph. I exaggerated wildly,

170

and turned the things I most loved to parody. I thought too quickly, and grew so impatient with my own sorrows that I turned them aside into laughter. I was so great a master of language that I thought I could fashion the world into my own image. In my days of purple and of gold, I did too many things too well. I had the openness of mind and the flexibility of intelligence which were the predominant notes of the Athenian people. I believed I was one such as Denys L'Auxerrois in Pater's story: the Greek boy born too late, who brought with him everywhere a mad joyfulness, one for whom the honours and injustices of the world were but light and trivial things. But, in reality, I courted success primarily. And that was to be my ruin. I remember reading, in my prison cell, Pascal's motto: 'Diseur de bons mots – mauvais caractère,' and I bowed my head at the justice of the indictment.

I was a vessel for the prose of the age, and in the end it flowed over my head. I revelled in its language but not in its morality and so, when I look back over my work, it sometimes has the strangely scented doom of hot-house flowers. Browning was not afraid to write an ugly line in order to express precisely his thought – that was his tragedy. I found meaning in beauty only and abjured ugliness – that was mine. I never saw reality. I put on a mask as easily as I adopted a mood, and as a result I became a prisoner of those masks and my moods; even now I am tempted to make *roulades* of phrases. Perhaps Frank was right: perhaps even in this journal I am not portraying myself as indeed I am. I feel like Timanthes who, despairing of his ability to represent Agammemnon's head, threw a drapery over it.

The doctor comes in half an hour: I must shave.

13 October 1900

I have been confined to bed: my doctor tells me that I am 'under observation'. I have explained to him that it is a position I am accustomed to.

Maurice arrived yesterday with Rowland Strong, a journalist for whom I have now become an object of curiosity. It is strange how people with the best of intentions always say the worst possible things. Strong seriously suggested that, to 'occupy yourself', in his immortal phrase, I should write a literary history of my age. I told him the age was immaterial. But surely I could write about my contemporaries? I have no contemporaries, I told him, I have only predecessors. He left in some dismay: I had not fulfilled the first duty of a sick man, which is to enliven one's visitors. His suggestion was ridiculous, however: if I look back upon those years in which I have lived and worked, I can see no history but only a series of accidents – some of them fatal.

As an age it was torn between Mrs Browning and Mrs Grundy, a desert in which only strange relics are found. I have never been interested in the work of my contemporaries, and I detest the critical mannerism that professes to find good in everything. Of the artists of my time, I admired Beardsley the most, although he never understood me. He was an *enfant terrible* playing monstrous games with adult passions, a mixture of innocence and lust, Sporus with a breviary in his hand. Dowson, too, I respected. Poor Dowson. He is dead now. He was born with an affliction, a sort of tenderness of the heart. It ruined his life and his poetry.

No, the only true artists of the period are now misty figures of the past. Pater and Ruskin are dead; Tennyson and Browning also, and I do not know if they will be able to survive their imitators. Swinburne and Meredith linger on, but in a half-light. No one has come to take their place, and it is most unlikely that anyone will. I might have done so but I betrayed my own gifts and,

172

in the weakness of my character, I found no great subject to redeem me.

Like everything else in the modern period, the decline has come too swiftly to be noticed or understood. In Latin there is a pause of some four hundred years from the magnificent prose of Claudian or Rufilius to the faded dialect of St Boniface or St Aldhelm. But the English, when engaged in destruction, work on the principles of speed and stealth: the means of proper expression have crumbled in a generation. We have gone from Tennyson to Kipling, from Meredith to Wells, so rapidly that even those trained to discern the difference have been able to perceive none.

But, like a dying star, English prose rose up in one last effort of glory before its fall – in myself, in Lionel Johnson and in Pater. But we were the individualists of art, and that was our weakness. Like Huysmans and Maeterlinck, we saw the ghosts of things, the pale chimaeras, the shadow of the rose upon the water. The pain is returning.

18 October 1900

I have written nothing new for some days. I cannot sleep or think. I am told that I must have an operation in four days' time – that I have an abcess in my ear which will affect my brain. I have sent a telegram to Robbie. I am in great fear. I want to live. I have so much more to say. Maurice will come with soup: I hope he has not cooked it himself.

28 October 1900

Operated on a few days ago. The doctor promises full recovery. I cannot write today.

11 November 1900

I had quite forgotten this little book. But now I have something to say, and I will talk to it.

Something has happened, something final. The operation has not removed the pain, it seems simply to have driven it underground where each day I search for it anxiously. And, when I woke this morning, I knew that the pain had finally taken hold. I have aged terribly and, for once, I do not need a mirror to show me: my body tells me quite plainly enough. I feel myself decaying – I want to scream out, but I cannot. I write now only with difficulty. Maurice leaves the journal by my bed. I rely upon Maurice so much now: he sits with me and, when I am awake, he reads to me. He wished to begin *Jude the Obscure*, but I begged him not to. It would add a new horror to the death-bed.

12 November 1900

I told the nurse who comes daily to dress the wound in my ear that I do not expect to recover. But he smiled and said nothing: I suppose it was wrong of me to expect him to have any concern for my physical welfare, since nurses never do. I would not mind death if it were not for the ugliness of those who minister to it. When I went last year to the dentist to have my teeth removed, the sight of the vice and the gas pump had no effect upon me. The real fright was the dentist – when I saw him, I called at once for anaesthesia.

14 November 1900

I am borne backwards, as if on the tide.

I used to swim a great deal once, but I do not suppose I shall do so again. Only in small matters can I glimpse the reality of what is happening to me. A mad letter arrived yesterday from a young man, Cowley or Crowley. It ended by assuring me that I would live for ever. This had been 'revealed' to him. I have never trusted revelation: it smacks of pessimism. I must pause now for I hear footsteps on the stairs. If it is not Death, it must be Maurice.

16 November 1900

Did I tell you that I have visited the Exhibition? It was in the spring. I was recognised in the American section – I thought that there at least I might pass, like everything else, as a curiosity – and a young man stopped me. He asked me to say something into Edison's speaking machine. Well, it did not speak to me, but then so few people do nowadays. I recited some lines from the *Ballad* and, as I did so, I felt chilled. I think that even then I had a premonition of my death. That place, and that machine, were not of my time.

I do not mind. I have seen too much already. The newspapers tell me that we are living in a period of 'transition' and for once they may be right. The old is shivered to fragments and no one, not even the journalists, knows what is taking its place. I could have been the voice of the coming age, for I proclaimed that which my age did not know – that every man should make himself perfect. But I was not understood: they perfected the bicycle instead. This is truly an age of iron.

It is too late now. If I am anything, I am a warning. I discovered, in my own tragedy, that artifice crumbles – an artificial world will dissolve also, and will have to face its own vacancy, as I did in a prison cell. And although my own century may have crushed me I am still nobler than my destroyer because I, at least, know that I must die.

The proprietor of the hotel, I cannot remember his name, asked me if this was the first year of the twentieth century or the last year of the nineteenth: I advised him to ask his children. Only they know.

179

17 November 1900

It is improbable, is it not, that anything I have said or done will survive me? Or perhaps I shall be a modern St Procopius, the torments of whose martyrdom were wonderfully increased by each succeeding legend until the time came when his relics healed the sick and opened the eyes of the blind: of course it was the legends that worked the miracles, not the bones.

On a Christian sarcophagus, on a martyr's tomb in Rome, Anatole France tells us that there is an inscription: 'Whatsoever impious man violates this sepulchre, may he die the last of his own people.' I have known the full weight of that curse – but also the strange joy which it brings. I must sleep now. I feel curiously apart from my writing, as though it were another hand which moves, another imagination I draw upon. Soon I must ask Maurice to take dictation from me: no doubt he will invent my last hours, and then the transition will be complete.

19 November 1900

He has been reading Balzac to me, although he professes not to understand it. I offer him a brandy-and-soda, and he becomes strangely interested. Now that my own life is quite remote from me, I long to enter the noisy thoroughfares and dilapidated courtyards of Balzac's imagination. The details of the past return and surround me, and I am at peace.

Maurice tells me that he does not care for 'old books', but I have explained to him that Balzac is the only thoroughly modern French novelist; he looked at me so sweetly that I knew at once that he did not believe me. I explained to him that the idea of progress is an absurdity: no age is to be preferred to another, and look, even I have become a child again. 'I will tell you a secret,' I said to him, 'I have told you that our age is primitive and terrible. Well, the next age will be primitive also, and then the next, and then the next.'

Dante walks in exile at the same time as Augustine speaks in the market place of Tyre, and Samson is led into the air by a boy. There is a picture of a young man in the Louvre – a prince, I believe, and his eyes are sad. I would like to see that picture again before I die. I would like to return to that past – to enter another man's heart. In that moment of transition, when I was myself and someone else, of my own time and in another's, the secrets of the universe would stand revealed.

22 November 1900

Robbie and More have come from England. Reggie arrives tomorrow: the three horsemen of my apocalypse. I told them that, if they were very good, I would share my chloral with them: it becomes interesting when it is mixed with champagne. I believe that they think I am simply posing as a dying man, and that tomorrow morning I will be patrolling the boulevards, on sentry duty as always. I explained to them that I am on very good terms with Death: he longs to visit, and leaves a fresh card each day.

I insisted that Robbie take me out. It was yesterday evening, I think. I felt unaccountably better. We did not get very far: the fiacre took us to a little café in the Rue de Rennes where strange dancers plead for *bock*. I must have been looking at everything very intently because Robbie asked me if I felt faint. I told him it was not faintness I was feeling, but wonder. Who would wish to leave the world when it has such people in it. 'You shall see the things I shall write now,' I told him. Then I broke down and wept. They took me back to my bed.

24 November 1900

Maurice has agreed to take dictation from me. I tell him that it will not be an arduous, or indeed a permanent, position – he turns away and is standing by the window now. I cannot bear this pain: the serpents are in my head. Never did De Quincey in all his laudanum dreams suffer as much as I do.

This is Oscar Wilde talking, taken down by Maurice Gilbert

26/11/1900

Bring me some champagne, *he says*, there's a good boy   *The doctor has put leeches on his temples but he does not feel them*

27/11/1900

There is something I want you to have, *he tells me*, there is in my possession an engraving of Faust sitting hunched at his desk, behind him there is a skeleton, a telescope and a mirror, do you think from this description you will be able to find it Maurice
He is sleeping now

28/11/1900

When he woke up he was in good spirits   When I die I shall probably get three inches in the Times under a German army officer that will no doubt be an extremely uncomfortable position   *He laughs with his high-pitched laugh. He asks me about Père Lachaise where I had gone with Mr Ross*   When you see three or four people gathered together around a grave, you know that there is a spirit within the world, Maurice. When God arrives to take me to his bosom, I shall turn around and say, 'Leave me alone. I am thinking.'   *He closes his eyes now. I think he is sleeping for the laudanum is very strong*   Well, things are as they are, don't you agree, Maurice? Perhaps I will have the pleasure of seeing myself die   *I tell him not to speak so*   I do not mind. I am only curious: I would like to know. It is the one sensation which has never been perfectly expressed. I have always hated that clock

29/11/1900

The nurse has come to inject him – I think with morphia although the doctor says not to. He is muttering to himself and I do not think it right to write it down, these are his own thoughts to himself. He turns to me and seems to recognise me for he points towards this book.   I saw beauty only. Without beauty there is nothing in the world, the beautiful is more than the good. I tried to catch it but even as I tried I fell deeper than any man
He is fading now. Mr Turner does not think he can last much longer and has gone to find a priest. Mr Wilde looks at me and says   I am ready, Maurice   *I do not know if he wants me to write or not*   I had fame without it I am smoke in the air and foam in the water. I am a great scandal, am I not?   *he laughs*
There was a great carp in Ireland, Maurice. It spoke to me once when I was a child. Do you know what it said? It said, I am asleep, little Oscar. Do not wake me. You will come to me one day, little Oscar. I heard the trees speak and the statues move.   *I think this is what he says*

30/11/1900

He is becoming delirious now but I will write it down for his words have always been wonderful to me
It has been a hot summer has it not   I tried to get a cab this morning but he said it was too far out. You know, when they found the body of Christ   *I cannot follow what he is saying here* and then once more I shall be lord of language and lord of life, do you agree, mother?   *he is laughing*   I knew I should create a great sensation   *no more now*

Mr Wilde died at ten minutes to two p.m. on Friday, November 30.

All Abacus Books are available at your bookshop or newsagent, or can be ordered from the following address: Abacus Books, Cash Sales Department, P.O. Box 11, Falmouth, Cornwall TR10 9EN.

Please send cheque or postal order (no currency), and allow 60p for postage and packing for the first book plus 25p for the second book and 15p for each additional book ordered up to a maximum charge of £1.90 in U.K.

B.F.P.O. customers please allow 60p for the first book, 25p for the second book plus 15p per copy for the next 7 books, thereafter 9p per book.

Overseas customers, including Eire, please allow £1.25 for postage and packing for the first book, 75p for the second book and 28p for each subsequent title ordered.